PATHWAY TO POWER

THE SPIRIT'S POWER FOR ABUNDANT LIVING AND ABOUNDING SERVICE

Michael A. Redick

nosnuma

PATHWAY TO POWER

Published by NOSNUMA International Pte. Ltd.

In sharing stories from other people's lives in this book, it has sometimes been necessary to change names and minor details to protect their privacy.

Designed by Kamal Gideon

All Scripture is quoted from The Holy Bible, King James Version

For Information:
NOSNUMA International Pte. Ltd.
96 Robinson Road, #05-02/03
SLF Building
Singapore 068899

TABLE OF CONTENTS

To my lovely and brilliant wife Lisa
for hours of tedious final editing ...

To my friend and brother Kamal Gideon,
whose creativity in work and life humbles me,
for the cover and book design and...

To Robert Wong, the visionary behind
NosNuma, who made sure the other two got
their work done ...

my thanks.

INTRODUCTION

In the last thirty years, our world has seen dramatic change. The computer chip, e-mail, and on-line buying have changed the way we live. Messages can be sent in an instant; books can be searched for, found, and purchased from the comforts of your own home. No generation has had greater access to more information. Satellites, fiber-optic cables, and television have made our world smaller—exporting and exposing culture to culture and slowly blending the world into one.

That same proportion of dramatic change has also gripped the church. Pragmatism has replaced purity; performance based ministry has replaced Spirit-filled preaching. When the world entered the church, the church lost its ability to impact the world, leaving Christians *struggling* with sin and the world *dead* in sin.

This change brought about an exchange; the church exchanged the God of the Word for the gods of this world. It exchanged the power of the Holy Spirit for the futility of the flesh, leaving the Christian empty and the church unable to reach its world. What the church has forgotten is that victory over sin and power in service is *"Not by might, nor by power, but by My Spirit, saith the Lord of hosts" (Zechariah 4:6). "The weapons of our warfare are not carnal, but mighty through God to the pulling down of strong holds" (II Corinthians 10:4).*

Our need today is not sensual and soulful music or a performance-based ministry. We do not need to change our structure, add more organization, improve our administration, or even advance ourselves in education. What is needed is the power of the Holy Spirit on what we already have. We need Spirit-filled musicians and messages. We need Spirit-filled preachers and Spirit-filled people. We need the power of the Holy Spirit in the pulpit and in the pew.

It is to this end that this book is written. Consistent victories over sin and courageous power in service are not the results of good organization, administration, or advanced education. They are not the products of pragmatism, performance-based ministry, or adding popular culture to our programs. Any and all success in our personal lives or in the church is the direct result of the Holy Spirit's power operating through Spirit-filled believers.

The message in this book presents a progression of truth leading the believer from defeat to victory, from a life of barrenness to a life of fruitfulness. Practical holiness and powerful service are the natural outflow of the Spirit-filled life. The ten chapters in this book present five themes that unfold the "Pathway to Power."

The Problem of Sin (Chapters 1–2)
Sin is the greatest hindrance to practical holiness and powerful service; therefore, we must be cleansed of sin.

The Provision of Christ (Chapters 3–4)
The work of Jesus Christ on the cross has made victory over sin and power in service possible; therefore, we must be Christ-centered.

The Preparation of Surrender (Chapters 5–6)
A yielded believer is a prepared vessel and is ready for the Master's use; therefore, we must be consecrated unto God.

The Power of the Spirit (Chapters 7–8)
The Holy Spirit is the agent who makes practical holiness and powerful service a reality; therefore, we must be controlled by the Spirit.

The Priority of Service (Chapters 9–10)
God uses only what He controls and He controls only those who are cleansed from sin, consecrated unto Him, and Christ-centered.

This is the "Pathway to Power" and the theme of this book. May all who read it step upon this pathway and experience the Holy Spirit's power.

Michael A. Redick

FOREWORD

Pathway to Power is simply that. In a logical Scriptural presentation, illustrated by numerous historical and personal experiences, Missionary Evangelist Redick graphically displays the great need for Bible believers in any age; that is, the power of God upon their lives, and then systematically lays a Biblical foundation to show how this power can be obtained.

Most of the Scriptural emphases he discusses were covered by numerous authors prior to 1950. However, the heavy onslaught of the excesses of the Charismatic movement in the second half of the twentieth century, has heavily impacted the true Scriptural teachings concerning the Spirit-filled and Spirit-controlled life and left many in darkness concerning the correct teaching of the Holy Spirit in relation to the believer.

It is a delight to see a new author go back to the old ways of the Scriptures and accurately interpret the doctrine of the Holy Spirit in such a practical manner that it becomes alive.

In a sin-saturated world exploding to over 6 billion people, God's people, whether in the pulpit or pew, need the power of God upon their lives more than ever before. Our enemies of the world, the flesh, and the Devil are maximizing every opportunity and seeking to mitigate our testimony for Christ.

The only Biblical answer to such an overwhelming flood of sin and enemies is the power of God. And this wonderful transforming power of God will not come apart from the Spirit-filled life.

The careful reading and the practical application of the truths in this volume will help you,the reader, to become more Christlike as you are Spirit-filled and know experientally the blessed power of God upon your life. Certainly that is well-pleasing to our Lord and gives significant merit to the efforts of the author.

Dave Sproul
General Director
International Baptist Missions

Life on Three Planes

I Corinthians 2:14–3:4

CHAPTER ONE

Life on Three Planes

I Corinthians 2:14–3:4

We read of the testimony of people like Hudson Taylor, who, by faith and with no promised financial support, evangelized Inland China and encouraged a thousand others to do the same. We read of D. L. Moody, who, though limited in education, personally won over one million souls to the Lord. We hear of the testimony of a chambermaid named Gladys Aylward, who, though small in stature and rejected by men, left England to serve God in China with absolutely nothing but the promises of God. We hear of the courage of John and Betty Stam, who gave their lives for the cross, and of the absolute surrender of Borden of Yale, who gave away millions of dollars to serve the Lord. We read of the boldness of Jim Elliot, who took the gospel to the most savage people on earth, and of the patience of James O. Fraiser, who labored among the Lisu for seven years before he saw his first convert. Whenever we hear of these testimonies, we immediately recognize men and women who lived their lives on a higher plane.

As we look about us, there is an obvious difference in the character and quality of the daily life of a Christians today. Some

Christians live joyful, radiant lives. The glory of the Lord seems to permeate their being. Others live and look as if they have spent their lives marinating in embalming fluid and drinking daily the juice of lemons and limes. Some Christians live consistent, climbing lives daily victorious over the Devil, the flesh, and the world. Others, instead of living in the sunshine of success, live in the shadow of defeat. In place of victory, there is defeat; instead of being victorious over sin, sin is victorious over them. Some Christians are stagnate in growth, while others superabound in growth. Some Christians live in the grip of selfishness, giving little of what they have to the work of the Lord while others sacrificially give much of what they have to prosper the work of the Lord. Some are fearless; they put their reputations on the line to witness, while others are fearful and will not witness whatsoever.

It is obvious that Christians live their lives on different spiritual planes. Not everyone lives on the same level. That which makes the difference, that which separates men, that which takes man from one level and one plane onto another is his willingness to receive, understand, and respond to spiritual truth. The Word of God is the touchstone, and the reaction to its truths automatically places a man on one of three spiritual planes.

In our passage, Paul, under the guidance of the Holy Spirit, divides the human race into one of three categories. Everyone finds himself on one of three spiritual planes. They are the natural man *(2:14)*, the spiritual man *(2:15–16)*, and the carnal man *(3:1–4)*.

There are two great spiritual changes that are possible in human experience: the change from the natural man to the saved man and the change from the carnal man to the spiritual man. The natural man becomes a saved man when he is rightly related to Christ. The carnal man becomes a spiritual man when he is rightly related to the Spirit. The natural man is saved when he receives, understands, and reacts to spiritual truth and casts his dependence on Christ to save him from sin and hell. The carnal man is spiritual when he receives, understands, and reacts to spiritual truth and casts his dependence on the Spirit to enable him to live victoriously in his Christian life.

It is possible to be saved and from that very moment to be so yielded to the Holy Spirit that you are spiritual. But that experience is not true of most Christians. The transition from the natural man to the saved man is made, but few make the transition from carnality to spirituality. Yet spirituality is God's divine ideal for man. Everyone lives on one of these three planes. On which do you live?

The Natural Man *(2:14)*

The first plane is that of the natural man. The natural man is the unsaved, unregenerate man. He has not been born again, so he is void of the Spirit of God. There are two primary characteristics of this natural man.

> *There are two great spiritual changes that are possible in human experience: the change from the natural man to the saved man and the change from the carnal man to the spiritual man.*

He Does Not Appreciate Spiritual Things (v. 14a)

The Scripture says, "*The things of the Spirit of God are*

foolishness unto him." In other words, spiritual things are meaningless to him. He has no "appetite" and no "appreciation" for spiritual things. My wife loves art. Whenever we are back in the United States, she loves to visit the Legion of Honor in San Francisco. Even though she has been there a dozen times, she always wants to go again. She tells me that the Legion of Honor has the largest collection of French art outside the Louvre in France. It is all arranged in chronological order, so she can move through the museum, avoiding certain periods. She can stand there transfixed before those giant masterpieces, spending hours slowly making her way through the museum. I, on the other hand, have absolutely no taste, no appetite, no appreciation for art whatsoever. To me the Legion of Honor is a nightmare, and it is one of my least favorite places to visit. The last time we were in San Francisco, I dropped my wife off at the Legion of Honor and went somewhere else. My idea of good art would be a well-stocked buffet table filled with all kinds of French pastries. When it comes to the arts, my wife's and my tastes lie in different directions.

The same is true of the natural man. He has no appetite for and no appreciation of spiritual things. Getting up early and going to church on Sunday rather than sleeping in and relaxing at home is crazy to him. Going to prayer meeting or attending a gospel service rather than going to see a movie or hanging out in a sports bar or karaoke lounge is absurd to him. The natural man has no appetite for or appreciation of spiritual things. He has no desire to go to church, read the Bible, live a holy life, give his free time in service to the church, or give a portion of his earnings to advance God's kingdom. His tastes lie in a different direction from those of the saved man.

He Does Not Apprehend Spiritual Things (v. 14b)

"Neither can he know them, because they are spiritually discerned." In other words, the natural man has no ability to know or understand the things of the Spirit. He is like a little baby in this physical world. He is like a blind man looking at the sunset or a deaf man listening to a symphony. He has no ability to know, to understand, or to apprehend those things. He is like a man who has never seen snow. You can tell him about water that gets so cold it freezes into little flakes which fall quietly to the earth and pile up until they soon cover the whole ground with a white powder of frozen water. But to him it is nonsense; he cannot understand and apprehend what he has not yet experienced. The same is true with the natural man. He may be brilliant and have a great mind; he may be able to understand the words of Scripture in their grammatical sense; he may be able to understand the geography, history, and ethical teachings of Scripture. But he can never understand nor truly communicate their spiritual content.

William Wilberforce, emancipator of Britain's slaves, was an earnest Christian. He was deeply interested in the salvation of William Pitt, the brilliant young man who became prime minister of England at age twenty-five. On one occasion Wilberforce persuaded Pitt to attend a drawing-room meeting at which Robert Cecil was the speaker. Wilberforce hoped that the meeting would result in Pitt's conversion. Wilberforce later said that he had never heard Robert Cecil preach with more power, logic, and unction than he did that night. As they left the gathering, Wilberforce asked Pitt how he liked Cecil's message. Pitt was silent for a moment, and then he replied, "To tell the truth, I gave Cecil my whole attention, but I was utterly unable to follow what he was driving at." [1]Pitt was sincere and brilliant, but he could not understand the things of the Spirit. He lacked the faculty by which spiritual truth is apprehended.

If a person can sit week after week listening to God's Word and still find it a mystery, and if he cannot understand what the preacher is "driving at", then that person is living on this natural plane. Spiritual truth is spiritually discerned. To understand spiritual truth, the natural man needs the Spirit; he needs to be born again. If a person has no appetite for and no appreciation of spiritual things, he is living on this natural plane. What he needs is to be born again. He needs to be rightly related to Christ. He needs to be saved. Salvation brings an appreciation and an apprehension of spiritual things.

The Carnal Man *(3:1–4)*

The second plane is that of the carnal man. The word *carnal* means "fleshly" and refers to one who lives his life on a purely human level. He is one who operates according to the flesh - one who lives his life for self rather than living it for God. The carnal man is a Christian, for Paul calls this man *"brethren" (3:1)*. By faith he is rightly related to Christ, but he is not rightly related to the Holy Spirit. Instead of living under the control of the Spirit, he lives under the control of the

If a person can sit week after week listening to God's Word and still find it a mystery, and if he cannot understand what the preacher is driving at, then that person is living on this natural plane.

flesh. This passage gives us five characteristics of a carnal Christian.

Stagnant in Growth (3:1)

These Corinthian believers were still *"babes in Christ."* They were still spiritual infants who had no excuse for their infancy. Most of these Corinthians had been saved for five years. Paul himself was their pastor for eighteen months. Apollos had been their pastor for several years, and according to *I Corinthians 1:12*, some of them had even sat under the teaching of Jesus Christ. But in spite of all the teaching and instruction in spiritual matters, they were still babes in Christ. The problem was not a low I. Q. or a lack of intelligence. It was the fact that they were carnal. They were so consumed with the world and its ways that they became forgetful hearers. When a person hears the Word and does not do what it says, he soon forgets what he has heard. Such an action is carnality. A carnal Christian is one who hears the Word but never grows spiritually. He sits week after week, year after year, and stagnates. He still struggles with the ABCs of the Christian life. He still has to be encouraged to do right, to read the Word, to pray, to come to church, and to witness. Where there is little or no growth, there is carnality.

Stubborn to the Truth (3:2)

"I have fed you with milk, and not with meat: for hitherto ye were not able to bear it." In a parallel passage we are told that these Corinthians did not receive spiritual truth because they were stubborn to it. *Hebrews 5:11* says they were *dull of hearing*. The word "dull" means "slow, sluggish, numb." In ancient literature the word "dull" characterized a mule. The primary characteristic of a mule is stubbornness. The reason

the Corinthians would not receive spiritual truth is that they were stubborn and mule-headed. This stubbornness is carnality.

We have all seen this mule-headed, stubborn, carnal Christian. He is the one who "knows it all." You cannot teach him anything. He says, "I have heard this before," and sits there with his arms folded daydreaming. He is the one who says, "Good message, but it was all review to me." He is the one who says, "Good message, Preacher. *They* really needed that." He is the one who says, "I can never get any truth from what he says; he does not feed me." Do you know what the problem is? Do you know why people are mule-headed to the truth? They do not want to do what it says. They do not want to quit doing what they are doing; they do not want to yield and surrender to God. So they make stubborn, mule-headed excuses, rejecting the truth.

Sinful in Habit (3:3a)

"For whereas there is among you envying, and strife, and divisions, are ye not carnal?" A carnal Christian is one who cannot get victory over sin. The sins he struggled with before he met Christ are the sins he struggles with today. Notice Paul asks, *"Are ye not carnal?"* In other words, are you still struggling with the same old sins? After all these years, can you still not get the victory? Are you still dealing with envy? Are you still dealing with strife and divisions? Five years later these Corinthians were still dealing with the same old sins. When pride and envy still dominate the life, when you cannot shake that bitterness or get victory over that temper, then your life is dominated by the flesh and not by the Spirit. It is a mark of carnality. If you are still dealing with the sins of yesterday today, then you are living in the flesh and not in

the Spirit. The carnal life is a life of defeat, a life of struggle; it is a life of little victory.

Secular in His Ways (3:3b)

"And walk as men?" When a Christian lives as an unsaved man, when he has the same desires and the same standards, when he enjoys the same things as the unsaved world, he is carnal. Several years ago I was listening to a Christian radio station. A leader of a major Christian organization began to share with the radio audience how the night before he and his wife had gone to see a wonderful movie. Then he began to encourage all those listening to go see it. The movie was *Titanic!* When a Christian can enjoy watching and listening to things that he knows God hates, such as nudity, vulgarity, God's name being taken in vain, and illicit sexual scenes, he is carnal. When our lives reflect the lives of the unsaved, whether in attitude, action, appearance, or in our entertainment, we are carnal.

Sectarian in Outlook (3:4)

"For while one saith, I am of Paul; another, I am of Apollos; are ye not carnal?" When men would rather follow men than follow God, when they follow a movement or a personality rather than following God and His revealed Word, when a man's loyalty is to a man above and beyond the truth, he is carnal. If your Christian life is characterized by spiritual stagnation with little or no growth, if you are stubborn to the truth, if you cannot find victory, if you find enjoyment in the things God hates, if you are more loyal to a man or to a movement than to God, you are carnal and are living life on the lowest Christian plane. The answer to the carnal life is the spiritual life.

The Spiritual Man *(2:15–16)*

The spiritual man is the exact opposite of the carnal man. He is all that the carnal man is not. The spiritual man is not only rightly related to Christ, but he is rightly related to the Holy Spirit. The spiritual man is simply a Spirit-filled man. He is one who lives his life for the purpose of pleasing God rather than self, and he does it under the power of the Holy Spirit. Notice several characteristics of a spiritual man.

Superabounds in Growth

If the carnal man is stagnant in growth, then the spiritual man is superabounding in growth. There is nothing static about his life. He has left behind the ABCs and is moving on to maturity. No longer does he have to be encouraged to come to church, to read the Word, to pray, to witness, and to do right. Now he is encouraging others; he is bringing others; he is teaching others to do right. He is growing in his Christ-likeness. He is producing "fruit, more fruit, and much fruit." His life is radiating those Christian graces of *Galatians 5:22–23*.

Submissive to Truth

If the carnal man is stubborn to truth, then the spiritual man is submissive to truth. The carnal man is stubborn to the truth because he does not want to do what it says. He wants his own way and his own will. He wants to govern his own life. But the spiritual man is submissive to the truth. He is surrendered to God. He wants God's will and God's way. Because of this, he will receive God's blessing.

When Evangelist Wilber Chapman was in London many years ago, he had the opportunity to meet General Booth of the

Salvation Army, who had just passed his eightieth birthday. The American evangelist asked General Booth the secret of his success. General Booth paused for a moment; then with a tear in his eye, he said, "I will tell you the secret; God has had all there was of me. There have been men with greater brains than I, men with greater opportunities; but the day I got the poor of London on my heart and a vision of what Jesus could do, I made up my mind that He would have all of William Booth there was. If there is any power in the Salvation Army, it is because God has all the adoration of my heart and all the power of my will and all the influence of my mind." Dr. Chapman went away from the meeting knowing "that the greatness of a man's power is the measure of his surrender."[2] The mark of a spiritual life is the submissive, surrendered life, and the surrendered life is the powerful, blessed life.

A young sixteen-year-old girl came to a meeting where the topic was victory in Christ. The young girl lived with a cantankerous aunt who was addicted to scolding. The girl often tried her aunt's patience by coming home late from school. When scolded for it, she always answered back. She went from the meeting determined to live victorious, and she told her aunt so. The skeptical aunt said she would believe in victory only when she saw it. A few days later, the young girl came home late again. The aunt took it as an opportunity to taunt her and said, "This is your victory, is it?" But not a word escaped the girl's mouth. A few days later, she wrote a letter to the speaker of the conference: "Oh, Miss Paxson, now I know the meaning of real victory, for when my aunt scolded me, I not only did not answer back, but I did not want to." [3] That is the victory of the spiritual man. It is a continuous, habitual victory over the outward action as well as the inward attitude of sin.

Separate in His Ways

To the spiritual man, the world with all its pleasures, pursuits, principles, and plans no longer exercises its power and its pull.

If the carnal man is secular in his ways, then the spiritual man is separate in his ways. The spiritual man is separated unto God and separated from the world. He can identify with Paul, who said in *Galatians 6:14, "The world is crucified unto me, and I unto the world."* The world with all its attractions has lost its charm, and the world with all its authority has lost its control. To the spiritual man, the world with all its pleasures, pursuits, principles, and plans no longer exercises its power and its pull. Jesus Christ is the center of his life and has complete control of his whole being. Jesus Christ dominates his thoughts, affections, speech, will, and actions. Jesus Christ is intensely real to the spiritual man. He considers, loves, serves, adores, and worships Him. The reason that the spiritual man is separate in his ways and loves Christ more than the world is that he yields himself unreservedly to the influence and operation of the Holy Spirit, through whom he has been enabled to seek, to receive, to love, and to know Jesus Christ.

Scriptural in His Outlook

If the carnal man is sectarian in his outlook, then the spiritual man is scriptural in his outlook. The spiritual man sees things through the looking glass of God's Word. The words, the ways, and the whims of man are no longer his final authority. Loyalty to the Lord is more important than loyalty to men. His outlook is scriptural, and he sees things from a scriptural point of view.

On which spiritual plane are you now living? If you find yourself on the natural plane, you need to be rightly related to Christ and that happens through the new birth. *John 1:12 says, "But as many as received Him, to them gave He power to become the sons of God, even to them that believe on His name."*

If you find yourself on the carnal plane, you need to be rightly related to the Holy Spirit. The Holy Spirit makes the spiritual life possible. You do not grow out of carnality into spirituality; you step out of it. Here is how. Acknowledge and admit to God your carnal condition *(I John 1:9)*. Abandon self and yield to the Savior *(Romans 6:13; 12:1)*. Accept the Spirit's filling by faith *(Galatians 3:2)*. Abide in Christ: abiding is not striving or struggling but simply obeying His will and ways *(John 15:4–5; I John 3:24)*. The Lord's promise is rivers of living water that flow from the Spirit-filled life *(John 7:38)*.

The Futility of the Flesh

Galatians 5:16–25

CHAPTER TWO

The Futility of the Flesh

Galatians 5:16-25

On September 11, 2001, four commercial jetliners took off from the East Coast of the United States. Unknown to the passengers and pilots aboard was an enemy who eventually revealed itself by hijacking the planes and guiding them like human missiles into the financial and military centers of the world's most powerful nation. The resulting deaths of several thousands of people from eighty different nations shocked the world. The aftermath caused stock markets to plunge, economies to slow, and unemployment lines to grow. The events of September 11, awakened the world to a new and ruthless enemy - an enemy that could strike anyone at anytime, anywhere. That enemy is called terrorism.

There is another enemy who is not as new but who is just as ruthless. As a matter of fact, it is this enemy who moved and motivated that vile act of terrorism. It is this enemy who fuels hatred and revenge, resulting in criminal activity. It is this enemy who hinders us from doing what we know we ought to do and keeps us from being what we ought to be.

This old and vile enemy is part of a network that has been terrorizing the world for thousands of years. The leader of this network is Satan, and his primary agent is the flesh. The flesh is the terrorist of the soul and what makes the flesh so effective is that it lives inside each and everyone of us.

Every believer has dwelling within him the flesh and the Spirit. The flesh we received at our natural birth; we inherited it from fallen Adam. The Spirit we received at our new birth. Both the flesh and the Spirit have desires - the flesh desires only evil and the Spirit desires only holiness. As a result, they are in conflict one with another. They are literally at war. Paul said, *"For the flesh lusteth against the Spirit, and the Spirit against the flesh: and these are contrary the one to the other: so that ye cannot do the things that ye would" (Galatians 5:17).*

If we yield ourselves to the rule and the reign of the flesh, then we will reap its evil desires and manifest its works in our life. But if we yield to the Spirit, we will reap His holy desires and manifest His fruit in our lives. It is for this reason that we must deny the flesh and depend upon the Spirit.

Every believer has dwelling within him the flesh and the Spirit. The flesh we received at our natural birth; we inherited it from fallen Adam. The Spirit we received at our new birth.

The Character of the Flesh *(v. 18)*

The word *flesh* is used in several different ways in the New Testament. Often it refers to our outer wrapper that keeps our bag of bones in place *(Galatians 2:20).* At other times, it refers to the

> *The flesh is our sinful patterns of living, the old habits, the old ways of thinking and acting.*

state of the unsaved man *(Romans 7:5)*. In our passage the word *flesh* is not referring to our physical body, our personality, or our spiritual state before God, but rather to our sinful patterns of living. The flesh refers to the old habits of life, the old ways of thinking and acting. The flesh is an entrenching evil principle of life, an established pattern of living that works in our members and wages war against the mind. As a result, we often end up doing the things we do not want to do *(Romans 7:22-23)*. It is the vehicle through which sin operates. In the Bible it is called *the body of sin (Romans 6:6) the carnal mind (Romans 8:7), the law of sin (Romans 7:23, 8:2)* and is referred to as an *evil* principle *(Romans 7:19)*. The flesh is the part of man that wants to please self rather than please God. The flesh is that part of you that rationalizes and justifies sin. Some say, "It was just a white lie, a little lie; it was a good lie; it was not a black lie or a big lie." That is rationalizing and justifying sin and that is the flesh. It is that part of you that wants its own way. It is that part of you that wants you to live apart from God. It is that part of you that moves you to do what you do not want to do. It is that part of you that leads you to argue, bicker, fight, and complain. It is that part of you that leads you into sin.

A little boy once asked his father, "How do wars begin?" "Well," said his father, "the First World War started when Germany invaded Belgium." Immediately, his wife interrupted him. "Tell the boy the truth. It began because somebody was murdered." The husband drew himself up in his chair with an air of superiority and snapped back, "Are you answering the question, or am I?"

Turning her back upon him in a huff, the wife walked out of the room and slammed the door as hard as she could. When the dishes stopped rattling in the cupboard, an uneasy silence followed, broken at length by the son when he said, "Daddy, you don't have to tell me anymore; now I know!"[1] That is the flesh. It is that part of you that drives you to sin.

The Flesh Desires Evil

Paul said in *Romans 7:21, "I find then a law* [law refers to a principle of life] *that, when I would do good, evil* [referring to the flesh] *is present with me."* In other words, when we desire to do good, this evil law, this evil principle of life, is there to oppose us. The desire of the flesh is purely evil. Its desire is to cause us to live independent of God. The flesh is so vile and so incurably evil that it cannot be educated or trained, nor can it be disciplined to change its character. The flesh will not respond to God or be subject to His laws *(Romans 8:7)*. The flesh is unable to do any spiritual good. There is no spiritual value in the flesh *(Romans 7:18)*. It cannot please God *(Romans 8:8)*. It cannot be trusted *(Philippians 3:3)*. It is a vile law that desires only evil.

The Flesh Defies God

Paul said in *Romans 8:7, "The carnal mind is enmity* [hostile] *against God: for it is not subject to the law of God, neither indeed can be."* The immediate response of the flesh to God is hostility. The natural response of the flesh to the Word of God is "No, never, not me!" Whenever we hear the Word of God and say, "No, never, not me! I will never respond to that truth. No, never, not me! I will never live like that. No, never, not me! I will never make that change," that is the flesh raising its ugly head against God. It is that evil, vile part of you that is hostile towards God.

The Flesh Defiles Man

The flesh pollutes man. It leads man to do the evil things that he does not want to do and keeps him from doing the good things he desires to do. That is why Paul said, *"For that which I do I allow not: for what I would, that I do not: but what I hate that do I . . . O wretched man that I am! who shall deliver me from the body of this death?" (Romans 7:15, 24).* The flesh pulls us into sin. The Devil takes the world's attractions, pursuits, and pleasures and appeals to our flesh, and our flesh tells us that the world is good. When pushed into a corner, the flesh says, "Fight, lie, cheat, steal, save face." Whenever the Spirit says, "Yes," the flesh says, "No." Whenever the Spirit says, "Run, flee, get out of there," the flesh says, "Stay, enjoy, indulge." The flesh is to the Devil what the Spirit is to Christ. The Spirit is in us to exalt Christ and to advance His kingdom. The flesh is in us to exalt Satan and to advance his kingdom. The Spirit corrects character, while the flesh corrupts character. The Spirit illumines truth, while the flesh ignores truth. The Spirit empowers us, while the flesh empties us. The Spirit counteracts sin, while the flesh cheers us on in sin. The flesh is Satan's agent and our adversary, and it has an all consuming desire to defile you.

The Flesh Destroys Life

Romans 8:13 says, *"For if ye live after the flesh, ye shall die."* Death is separation. However this passage is not referring to an eternal separation from God in hell, for the passage is addressing Christians. The desire of the flesh is to separate us from God unto Satan. Its desire in our life is to separate us from serving God to serving self, to separate us from having consistent victory to having continual defeat, to separate us from depending on God's power to depending on ourselves for power and thus destroying our spiritual lives.

That is the character of the flesh. It is our sinful patterns of living that are hostile to God, that wants us to live independent of God, that leads us to do what we do not want to do, and that brings us to spiritual ruin.

The Conduct of the Flesh *(vv. 19-21)*

When we do not deny the flesh and fail to depend upon the Holy Spirit, the life will begin to manifest the works of the flesh. The works of the flesh can be divided into three categories: sexual sins, superstitious sins, and social sins. This list is not exhaustive, but rather a sampling of what happens when one chooses to live according to the flesh instead of according to the Spirit.

Sexual Sins (v. 19)

Adultery is the first of sexual sins. This refers to sexual sin between married people. It is not just the physical act that makes one an adulterer. Jesus said, *"Ye have heard that it was said by them of old time, Thou shalt not commit adultery: But I say unto you, That whosoever looketh on a woman to lust after her hath committed adultery with her already in his heart" (Matthew 5:27-28).* It is not just the outward action that makes one an adulterer; it is the inward attitude of the heart. When a married person involves himself with another that is not his spouse, whether he involves himself physically (the act of sex), mentally (lust or fantasy), or emotionally (verbal intimacy), he is guilty of adultery.

Fornication is any and all illicit sexual activity. The word fornication comes from the Greek word *pornia*, from which we get the English word *pornography*. It seems that Satan's greatest attack today is in the realm of sex. The primary vehicle that Satan uses to fuel the flesh is pornography. Today in America there are more hard-core pornography outlets than McDonald's restaurants. In addition, eighty percent of the more than twenty-six thousand video shops sell pornography. Pornography generates more money than rock and country music combined and more than Hollywood's box office receipts, making it a twelve billion dollar a year business. People today do not even have to leave the comforts of their own homes to view pornography. The Internet brings it right into their bedrooms. Over twenty percent of Americans have viewed pornographic websites.[2] This is the work of the flesh.

Uncleanness is filthy thoughts.

Lasciviousness is sensuality and refers to a shameless display, such as nudity or immodest dressing.

When the flesh is allowed to rule, it can lead even the best Christian into any one of these sins. The 1988 winter issue of Leadership Magazine polled one thousand pastors and found that twelve percent admitted they had committed adultery while in the ministry and twenty-three percent felt they had done something considered sexually inappropriate. When the same questions were asked of Christians, twenty-three percent admitted to adultery, and forty-five percent admitted to inappropriate sexual behaviour.[3] This is the work of the flesh.

Superstitious Sins (v. 20)

Idolatry is the first in the category of superstitious sins. This is worshipping anything or anyone other than God. It is putting something before God. Anything can be an idol. We often drive idols; we call them cars. We often live in idols; we call them homes. We often spend idols; we call it money. We often wear idols; we call them clothes. When any one of these takes priority over God, the flesh is dominating.

Witchcraft is the same word translated *sorcery*, and it is the Greek word *pharmakeia*, from which we get the English word *pharmacy*. It refers to drug use. When an individual takes mood or mind-altering drugs, whether those drugs are taken for pleasure, to escape reality, to forget the past, or just to relax, it is an indicator that the flesh is dominating.

Social Sins (vv. 20b-21)

Hatred is the first of social sins, which is *antagonism towards another*. Hatred leads one to say, "I cannot stand that person; I will not be around him."

Variance refers to a quarrelsome person, one who is not easy to get along with. A quarrelsome person is "touchy" and argues at the slightest provocation. He is explosive. We would call him hot-tempered. He is the guy who slams the door or storms out of the room in a huff and a puff. He is the guy behind you at the stoplight who blows his horn the moment the light turns green, pulls up alongside you to give you the stare of death, and then gives his car the gas, only to beat you to the next stoplight by mere seconds.

Emulation is jealousy. It simply causes one to want what others have. It causes one to be upset when someone else gets greater recognition than he does. He becomes furious and vows to quit his job when someone else gets the promotion he had expected to receive. An old fable tells the following story: Satan's agents were failing in their attempts to draw into sin a holy man who lived as a hermit in the desert of Northern Africa. Every attempt was met with failure. So Satan, angered with the incompetence of his subordinates, became personally involved in the case. He said, "The reason you have failed is that your methods are too crude for one such as this. Watch this." He then approached the holy man with great care and whispered into his ear, "Your brother has been made the Bishop of Alexandria." Instantly, the holy man's face changed; a great scowl formed over his mouth, and his eyes tightened, and Satan knew he had won the victory.

Wrath refers to an outburst of anger. An example of wrath is a father who gets upset and throws a chair across the room, or a mother who slaps her child across the face, or a teenager who does not get his way and storms out of the room, or a child who throws himself on the floor, screaming and yelling to get what he wants.

Strife refers to disputes. A person characterized by strife is one who returns argument for argument. He says, "They argued with me, so I argued with them."

Sedition and factions refer to a group of people who band together and take sides. Instead of saying, "I am for truth," they say, "I am for him." When people cannot get along and make things right, when people want to split and divide, this is a mark of the flesh.

Envy is another form of jealousy.

Murder is taking the life of another or self-murder (taking one's own life.)

Drunkenness is being intoxicated with alcohol.

Revelling is being boisterous and loud, usually due to the use of alcohol.

This is the conduct of the flesh. This is what happens when we allow the flesh to rule and reign in our lives. Every one of us is capable of committing each of these sins. No one can say, "No, not me. Maybe I could commit some of the social sins but not the sexual sins." Very few people get up in the morning and plan to sin. These sins are not the planned actions of the Christian. I do not believe that King David got up in the morning and said, "I think I will commit adultery with Bathsheeba and then have her husband Uriah killed." I do not think Noah after work one day said, "I think tonight I will get drunk and then lay in my tent naked for all to see." I do not think that Peter planned to deny the Lord and then curse His name on the night of His arrest. I do not think these men planned to do these things, but their conduct is a picture and a reminder of what can happen when even the best of men yield to the flesh rather than to the Spirit.

The Consequences of the Flesh *(v. 21b)*

> *Those who live according to the flesh will not receive their full possession in the kingdom of God. They will forfeit many blessings and benefits available to believers.*

What are the consequences of living under the reign and rule of the flesh? Paul says, *"They which do such things shall not inherit the kingdom of God."* In this passage Paul is addressing Christians, and he is warning them that those who do such things will forfeit their inheritance in the kingdom of God. The word *inherit* means *"entering into full possession of."*[4] Those who live according to the flesh will not receive their full possession in the kingdom of God. They will forfeit many blessings and benefits available to believers.

Paul did not say, "Those who live according to the flesh and manifest the works of the flesh shall not enter the kingdom of God." Nor did he say, "Those who do such things will lose their salvation." Salvation is not based on what we do or on what we do not do; it is not based on living a good life. Paul did not say, Those who live according to the flesh are giving evidence that they are not saved. However, Paul did say, those who do such things will not enter into the full possession of their heavenly inheritance. He is not dealing with our sonship but with the son's inheritance.

Our inheritance is the reward for faithfully serving Christ. *Colossians 3:23-24* makes this clear. *"And whatsoever you do, do it heartily, as to the Lord, and not unto men; Knowing that of the Lord ye shall receive* ***the reward of the inheritance****: for ye serve the Lord Christ."* When people live according to the flesh, they are robbing themselves of their heavenly reward. They are forfeiting their inheritance - the blessings and benefits available to the child of God and they will suffer loss. *I Corinthians 3:15*, speaking of the carnal believer, says, *"If any man's work shall be burned, he shall suffer loss: but he himself shall be saved; yet so as by fire."*

He will suffer the loss of Christian fellowship and service. *I Corinthians 5:11* says, *"But now I have written unto you not to keep company, if any man that is called a brother be a fornicator, or covetous, or an idolater, or a railer, or a drunkard, or an extortioner; with such an one no not to eat."*

He will suffer loss by way of chastisement. *Hebrews 12:6* says, *"For whom the Lord loveth He chasteneth, and scourgeth every son whom He receiveth."* The Lord chastens with family tragedy, an early death, physical sickness, or perhaps financial loss. Although living in the flesh is possible, it is not very pleasurable.

He will suffer loss at the judgment seat of Christ. *Romans 14:12* says, *"So then every one of us shall give account of himself to God."* He who has lived his life in the flesh and who has lived independently of God and His claim upon his life will suffer loss. He will suffer the loss of praise; Christ will not say to him, "Well done, my good and faithful servant." He will suffer loss of possession; Christ will not reward him with the crowns of faithfulness, soul winning, and righteousness. He will suffer the loss of position; Christ will not invite him to occupy a place of authority in His kingdom.

A man can live according to the flesh, but he will suffer loss. The flesh is a vile, ruthless enemy. Its desire is to ruin you and to rob you of your heavenly inheritance.

The Conquest of the Flesh *(vv. 16, 18, 24-25)*

How can we get victory over the flesh? How can we deny this vile, evil enemy that brings such horrible consequences? The only answer to the flesh is the Spirit. It is the Holy Spirit who leads us to victory.

Yield to the Spirit's Leadership

We deny the flesh when we choose to follow the leadership of the Holy Spirit. To follow the leadership of the Holy Spirit, we must first be *led of the Spirit (v. 18)*. The word "led" refers to a shepherd leading his sheep or a farmer herding his cattle or a ship being driven by the wind. Just as a shepherd leads the sheep or the wind drives a ship, so the Spirit of God is to lead us. The Holy Spirit leads us by placing His desires in our hearts. He leads us by asserting His desires against the desires of the flesh.

When the flesh says, "Yes, do it, say it, think it," then the Spirit says, "No, do not do it, do not say it, do not think it." That is the leadership of the Holy Spirit. That is the Holy Spirit showing you the way of escape. That is the Spirit leading you to victory. Victory begins when we yield to the Spirit's leadership and obey His voice.

Walk in the Spirit's Way

Not only must we yield to the leadership of the Holy Spirit, but we must also *"walk in the Spirit" (v. 25)*. The word *walk* means to walk in step with the Spirit. It means to follow His leadership. Victory over indwelling sin comes when we yield to the Spirit's control and walk in His way. When you are in conversation with someone and the flesh says, "Let him have it!" and the Spirit says, "No, do not respond in that way," victory comes when you choose to follow His leadership and walk in that direction. The moment you choose to step in the direction of the Spirit's leading, at that moment you will receive the Spirit's power to enable you to walk in that direction. Victory over the flesh is thus given.

When we deny the flesh the right to rule and reign by choosing instead to yield to the Holy Spirit's leadership and to walk step-by-step in that direction, then every step we take is an act of dependence upon the Spirit and every act of dependence brings the enabling power of God, which brings moment-by-moment victory over the flesh. This is the promise of God. *"This I say then, Walk in the Spirit, and ye shall not fulfill the lust of the flesh" (v. 16).*

The choice is ours. We can live in the futility of the flesh, manifesting the works of the flesh, and be defiled, defeated, and spiritually destroyed. Or we can choose to walk in step with the Spirit, manifesting His fruit and finding victory and life. Will you deny the flesh by choosing to follow the leadership of the Holy Spirit?

CHAPTER three

Wanted Dead and Alive

Romans 6:1-14

CHAPTER THREE

Wanted Dead and Alive

Romans 6:1-14

In the town in which I was raised, there is a little post office. As a boy I loved to go there to look at the FBI's most-wanted list. I would read the names and the crimes and look at the faces of those who were considered America's most wanted. My hope was that one day I would spot one of these criminals, be able to turn him in, and receive the reward. These men and women, having already been convicted of crimes, were so dangerous to society that the government had put in large letters above the pictures of their faces the words "Wanted Dead or Alive."

Romans chapter six is God's wanted poster. However, God is not looking for criminals. He is looking for Christians. He does not want us "dead or alive." He wants us "dead and alive"-that is, dead to sin and alive to Him. God's way is the only way to true victory. It is the only way to have victory over the power of sin.

Sadly, many Christians, having been freed from the penalty of sin, have not yet found victory over the power of sin. Instead of living in the love, joy, peace, longsuffering, kindness, gentleness, goodness, and faithfulness of the Holy Spirit, they

Sadly, many Christians, having been freed from the penalty of sin, have not yet found victory over the power of sin.

continue daily to fall into the sins of the flesh. They are like Lazarus who, having been dead four days when Jesus called him forth from the grave, came out of the tomb still wrapped from head to toe in all his old grave clothes. When Jesus saw this, He ordered those standing by to unbind him and set him free *(John 11:44)*. What a vivid picture of many believers who, having been made spiritually alive at salvation, are still bound in the grave clothes of their old sinful lives. They are still carrying on the old habits, holding to the old attitudes, and following the old way of doing things - seeking victory but finding only defeat.

What many fail to realize is that victory over sin is not found in self-determination, self-discipline, or self-denial; nor is it found in the surrender of self. Victory over sin begins when we become aware of and appropriate the reality that we are dead to sin and alive in Christ. Our passage details clearly how we can live free from the power of sin.

An Awareness of Our Position in Christ *(vv. 1-10)*

When Jesus Christ died on the cross, He died as our substitute. He died for us, setting us free from the penalty of sin. But not only did Jesus die *for* us, He also died *as* us, identifying Himself with us and setting us free from the power of sin and giving us a new position in Christ. An awareness of this truth is the beginning and the basis of our victory.

We Are One with Christ (vv. 3-5)

Because Christ died for us and as us, we are one with Christ. The word "baptize" in verse 3, pictures this oneness. Baptism as used here does not refer to our water baptism. It refers to our Spirit baptism. It refers to the day of our salvation *(I Corinthians 12:13)*. When we trusted Christ as Savior, the Holy Spirit immediately immersed us into Christ, and at that very moment we became one with Him. The Holy Spirit took us and identified us with everything Christ did for us. All that Jesus Christ achieved in His death and resurrection became ours. God sees everything that happened to Christ as having happened to us. Which means when Christ died, we died. We shared His death. When He arose from the grave, we arose with Him. We are participants in all that Jesus Christ did for us. Salvation totally identified us with Christ, making us one with His death and resurrection.

During the American Civil War, the United States government drafted a man by the name of George Wyatt to go to the front of the battle. Wyatt had a wife and six children. A young man named Richard Pratt offered to go in his place. Pratt was accepted and joined the ranks of the army bearing the name George Wyatt. Before long Pratt was killed in action. The government later again sought to draft George Wyatt into service. However, he protested entering the plea that he had died in the person of Richard Pratt. The government consulted the records and eventually exempted him from any further military service. The reason given for this exemption was the fact that George Wyatt was dead; he had died in the person of Richard Pratt. In the eyes of the government, George Wyatt was both dead and alive.

The same is true of us. When we trusted Jesus Christ as Savior, we died in the person of Jesus Christ. We died to the old life and were raised to walk in newness of life with Christ *(v. 4)*. In the eyes of God we are both dead and alive. We are dead to sin *(vv. 2-3)* and alive in Christ *(v. 4)*. The power to walk in the newness of life begins when we are aware of the fact that we are both dead and alive - that we are one with Christ *(v. 4)*.

We Are Dead to Sin (vv. 1-2, 6-8)

When we asked Christ to save us, not only were we identified with Christ but also with the old man. The old Adamic nature was crucified; it was put to death. In verse 6, Paul says, *"Knowing this, that our old man is crucified with Him."* Crucifixion of the old man is not something we do; it refers to something that has already been done. It refers to an action that has happened in time past. When Jesus Christ was crucified, our old nature was crucified with Him.

This is a common teaching in the Scripture. In *Ephesians 4:22*, Paul says, *"Ye put off concerning the former conversation the old man."* And in *Ephesians 4:24*, he says, *"Ye put on the new man."* He was not telling us here to do something. The words *put on* and *put off* are infinitive of result, which refers to something that has already been done. Paul is stating a fact; he is not giving a command. The same is true in *Galatians 2:20*, which says, *"I am crucified with Christ."* He is not telling us to go out and crucify ourselves or to flog ourselves or to practice some type of self-mutilation to free ourselves of sin. He is stating a fact; he is reminding us that the old man, the old sinful nature, has already been crucified. Again in *Colossians 3:5*, the phrase *mortify therefore your members* can be better understood as *"consider as dead your members"* (NASB).

What does it mean "that our old man is crucified?" It means that sin has been rendered inoperative in our lives. In verse 6, the word *destroyed* means "to make ineffective." That is exactly what happened when we were united with Christ. Sin's rule and reign were broken. Sin lost its power, its control, and its authority in our lives. It means that the flesh, the Devil, and the world are no longer our masters. We are no longer their slave. It means we are free to choose not to sin *(vv. 6-7)*. It means when sin knocks at the door of our lives, we do not have to open the door and let sin in. It means we are no longer obligated to sin; we are no longer bound to do as sin commands.

Suppose, for example, you are renting an apartment and your landlord is a miserable man who delights in making your life just as miserable. He charges exorbitant rent; he barges into your apartment unannounced; he scolds and nags you for the way you keep the apartment. Then one day a new owner buys the apartment building. He is a new kind of landlord: friendly, fair, and even allows you to live in the apartment free of charge. Sometime later the old landlord comes to your door, and he is as mean as ever. He threatens you and reminds you that since you rented from him for so many years you are still obligated to obey him. What would you do? You would remind him that at the same time he lost ownership of the building, he lost authority and power in your life. You are freed from any and all obligations to him.

When we trusted Christ as Savior, at that moment we were identified with Him. As a result, sin lost its ownership, its control, and its authority in our lives.

That is our relationship to sin. When we trusted Christ as

Savior, at that moment we were identified with Him. As a result, sin lost its ownership, its control, and its authority in our lives. We do not have to open the door when sin knocks and asks to be let in. Each of us could open the door if we wanted to, but we do not have to. Sin has no independent authority in our lives; sin cannot twist our arm and make us move in its direction. We have been set free. If we sin, it is not because we have to, but because we make the choice to do so. We are one with Christ and dead to sin.

We Are Alive in Christ (vv. 9-10)

Not only are we one with Christ and dead to sin, but we are also alive in Christ. Our salvation identified us with Christ's death and resurrection. Christ defeated the penalty of sin, broke the power of sin, and placed His power within us, thus empowering us to walk in the newness of life *(v. 4)*, to say "No!" to sin *(v. 9)*, and to live unto God *(v. 10)*. Victory begins when we are aware of our position in Christ. It is being aware of the fact that we are one with Christ; we are dead to sin and alive in Christ.

There was once two Irishmen named Pat and Mike who found a most unusual turtle. The poor animal's head had been completely severed from its body. The turtle, however, was still moving around as if nothing had happened. Pat maintained that the turtle was dead; Mike insisted the turtle was alive. As they discussed the issue, they began to argue. Then O'Brien came along. They decided that he should give the final verdict. As he looked at this remarkable turtle, he said, "It is dead, but it does not know it."[1] That is where victory begins, with an awareness that we are both dead to sin and alive unto God.

An Appropriation of Our Provision in Christ *(vv. 11-12)*

After reading the first five and one-half chapters in the book of Romans, we come to the first verse in which we are told to do something. This is the first exhortation. Up to this point in the book, everything has been information. But in verse 11, we are told to *"reckon ye also yourselves to be dead indeed unto sin, but alive unto God through Jesus Christ our Lord."* The word *reckon* is a bookkeeping term and means "to impute to one's account" or "to count on a fact as being true."

Suppose a businessman were to say to his accountant, "What is the total amount needed to meet this month's payroll?" After some calculation the bookkeeper says, "Twenty thousand dollars, sir, but there's a balance of only five thousand dollars in our account right now." "Make out the checks," the businessman might say, "but do not give them to the men until you hear from me." Then the businessman calls his banker, arranges for a loan of thirty thousand dollars, calls his accountant, and says, "You can now pass out the checks. The bank has more than covered the payroll." Presently the first employee calls at the office for his paycheck. "I'm sorry," says the accountant, "I cannot let you have your check right now. The total payroll is twenty thousand dollars, and there is only five thousand in the bank. Here you can look at the ledger and see for yourself." What would the accountant be failing to do? He would be failing to reckon; he would be failing to take into account that adequate provision had been made to meet the needs of the payroll.[2]

That is what is means to *reckon.* It is being aware of the fact that Christ has made adequate provision for you and depending on this fact to be true. To reckon is an act of faith; it is taking

Only when we accept the fact that we are both dead and alive, by faith appropriating this fact, will we see any measure of victory over sin.

God at His word. Only when we accept the fact that we are both dead and alive, by faith appropriating this fact, will we see any measure of victory over sin. Victory is realized when the fact is appropriated by faith.

Appropriation Terminates the Dominion of Sin (v. 11a)

Some may argue, saying, "But I do not feel like the dominion of sin has been terminated. How can I reckon what I do not feel?" Faith is not based on feeling; it is based on God's Word. We reckon ourselves to be dead indeed unto sin because God said it and God cannot lie. We may not feel dead, but that does not change the fact. We may set the alarm to ring at six o'clock in the morning and when it goes off, sit up in bed and say, "It does not feel like six o'clock." But our feelings do not change the fact.

The fact is we are dead to sin, and whenever we are tempted to sin, we can appropriate this truth. In faith we can say, "Lord Jesus, I feel self rising; nail it," and that is what He does. Jesus takes the ugly, old self and nails it to the cross. When we feel our temper rising, we can say, "Kill it, Lord." And that is exactly what He does. He comes by way of the Holy Spirit and slays those passions, giving us instant victory. When we sense an old, sinful habit knocking at the door, we can cry out in faith, "Put it to death, Lord." And that is what He does. He, by faith, imputes victory to our account.

Appropriation Empowers for Holy Living (v. 11b)

Flowing from Calvary is a double stream - a stream of death terminating the dominion of sin and a stream of life empowering us for holy living. When we are faced with a difficult task or confronted with some new demand upon our life or ministry, we must then reckon ourselves *alive unto God.* And at that very moment, we will be infused with His divine life and enabled by His divine power. We will find Christ absolutely adequate to meet our every need.

Years ago a South African millionaire bought a Rolls Royce. So impressed was he with the car that he wanted to know everything about it. He asked the agent about every detail, including the horsepower. The agent gave him all the information he could, except for the horsepower. The agent explained, "We are not allowed to divulge this information; and in any case, I do not know the answer." The millionaire insisted on knowing, so the agent proposed to investigate the matter further. He telegraphed London and gave all the specifications of this particular car and then asked them to wire the information concerning the horsepower. A brief time elapsed, and then the telegram signed by Rolls Royce came back to the agent. The message had one word: *Adequate.*[3]

When you are faced with the problems of everyday life, when you are under a heavy load of burdens or stress, when your marriage is about to collapse, appropriate Christ's life; reckon yourself *alive unto God.* You will find the power of Christ absolutely adequate for your every need.

An Abandonment of Our Person to Christ *(vv. 13-14)*

Although the rule and reign of sin has been broken and it is no longer our master and we are no longer its slave, still sin remains a restless and relentless dethroned monarch seeking to recapture the throne of your life. In order to maintain victory over the power of sin, we must know that we are both dead and alive, by faith reckon this to be true, and then continually yield ourselves to God.

Abandonment Begins with a Decision (v. 13)

The word *yield* means "to surrender, to abandon." But what are we to surrender? We are to surrender *"ourselves to God."* This includes the body, the hands, the feet, the eyes, the ears, the tongue-the entire being is to be surrendered to God. Two times the word yield is used in this passage. The first time the word is used in the present tense and refers to a continual attitude of surrender. The second time the word is used refers to an initial act of surrender. It refers to a "once-and-for-all" decision we make to abandon ourselves to Christ. Have you made the initial decision to yield yourself to God? And if so, are you constantly yielding yourself to God?

When a family invites you into its home, your freedom in that home is often very limited. You are free to sit in the living room and perhaps step into the kitchen or use the bathroom. But if the couple gives you the keys to the house and says, "The house is yours to use; come and go as you please; make this home your own," you would feel great liberty for the whole house-every room, every cupboard, every drawer-would be yours. That is what Christ wants from us. He wants the key to every room of our life. He wants us to yield every room and then to continually yield that room. He wants us to open every door of our lives to Him and then keep that door open. He wants complete and total access.

One reason so many Christians have so little victory over sin is that they have not *initially* surrendered every room and then *continually* surrendered every room. They have not given Christ the key to every door, every cupboard, and every drawer in their lives. Some still hold onto the keys of pride, anger, selfishness, lust, and unforgiveness, locking them behind closed doors unwilling to give them up. Victory demands that these doors be opened and remain open.

Do you realize that we do not have to obey sin's impulses and its pull? We are free to refuse and to say no. Any authority that sin has in our lives is a given authority. We sin because we yield ourselves to the flesh and not to God. People sin because they yield the tongue to gossip, the eyes to lust, the hands to deception, and the body to immorality. Victory demands that we yield ourselves to God, and this begins with an initial decision, a choice to abandon ourselves to God.

Abandonment Brings with It Deliverance (v. 14)

"For sin shall not have dominion over you." This is a promise, an absolute certainty. If we are aware of our position in Christ and appropriate that provision and choose to yield ourselves to God, we can anticipate daily deliverance and continual victory over indwelling sin.

In Washington, D.C., stands the Vietnam Veterans Memorial. Etched in the black, clear granite wall are the names of 58,156 Americans who gave their lives in the war. Since its opening in 1982, the monument has stirred deep emotion. Some visitors walk its length slowly, reverently, and without pause. Others stop before certain names remembering a son, a sweetheart, or a fellow soldier. Some wipe away tears or trace the names with their fingertips. Among the names of those remembered can be found those of three veterans who could this day walk up to the wall and find their own names carved into the stone. Because of a data-coding error, each of them was incorrectly listed as killed in action. They are dead but alive.[4] This is how God wants us-dead to sin and alive unto Him.

Victory over sin begins by being aware of our position in Christ. It is realized by appropriating our provision in Christ, and it is maintained by abandoning our person to Christ.

The Pathway to Victory

Galatians 2:20

CHAPTER FOUR

The Pathway to Victory

Galatians 2:20

Not long ago, I had the joy of teaching a class on the aims of the Christian life. I mentioned ten different aims that are set forth in the Word of God. As Christians, we aim to walk as Jesus walked *(I John 2:6)*, to love our enemies *(Matthew 5:44)*, to forgive as Jesus forgave *(Colossians 3:13)*, to give thanks for all things *(Ephesians 5:20)*, to worry about nothing *(Philippians 4:6-7)*, to rejoice in the Lord always *(Philippians 4:4)*, to be blameless and without rebuke *(Philippians 2:15)*, to live abundantly *(John 10:10)*, to be free from the dominion of sin *(Romans 6:6-7)*, and to be in all things more than conquerors *(Romans 8:37)*. After explaining each aim in detail, I asked the question, "Are these aims actual possibilities? Are they attainable?" Sadly, the entire class answered, "No, these aims are not attainable." I fear that the people in this class were neither unique nor alone in thought. If others were asked the same question, they would likely give the same response.

There are many that look at the Christian life and the Word of God as a series of demands that cannot be fulfilled, conduct that cannot be reached, and goals that cannot be achieved. My wife was once talking to a group of ladies about living the victorious Christian life. In the course of the discussion, a lady asked the question, "How do you get victory over anger?" Immediately another lady spoke up and said, "You must just practice self-control. It is all right to be angry on the inside as long as you do not show it on the outside." To which my wife strongly disagreed, saying, "That is not victory. True victory not only does not get angry, it does not want to." The lady immediately protested, saying, "That kind of victory is not possible." Her reason? She argued that she had never met anyone who lived like that. Her response reminds me of an old Quaker lady who apparently never lost her temper and who remained unruffled even under the most trying circumstances. One day she was approached by a young girl, who said, "Please tell me how you keep sweet the way you do. If some of the things that happened to you happened to me, I would just boil over. But you never do!" The old Quaker lady said quietly, "Perhaps I do not boil over, but you do not see what boiling is going on in the inside."

God is not in the practice of making demands upon His children that cannot be fulfilled. He does not expect conduct that is beyond our reach. If God has set the standard, then the standard is achievable.

One reason so few have true victory is that they do not believe victory is possible. Thankfully, God is not in the practice of making demands upon His children that cannot be fulfilled. He does not expect conduct that is beyond our reach. If God has set the standard, then the standard is achievable. If God says, *"Let all bitterness, and wrath, and anger, and clamour, and evil speaking, be put away from you". (Ephesians 4:31)*, it is possible. If God says that He can always lead us in triumph *(II Corinthians 2:14)*, it is possible. If God says, *"Love your enemies, bless them that curse you, do good to them that hate you, and pray for them which despitefully use you, and persecute you" (Matthew 5:44)*, it is possible. If God tells us to walk as He walked *(I John 2:6)*, then it is possible. If God tells us to worry about nothing *(Philippians 4:4-7)*, it is possible.

But the question is how? How is this kind of victory possible? How can we live this kind of life? The answer is found in *Galatians 2:20*. This text paves the way for us to follow the pathway to true victory.

The Authority of the Cross *(v. 2:20a)*

The authority of the cross is seen in this phrase: *"I am crucified with Christ."* When you put your faith in Jesus Christ, you are immediately freed from the penalty of sin, and at the same time you are freed from the power of sin.

Crucifixion with Christ Is a Fact

When Paul says, "I am crucified with Christ," he is not telling us to do something. He is referring to something that has already been done. He is referring to an action that happened in time past. When Jesus Christ was crucified, our old Adamic nature (that old man) was crucified with Him. The old man and the old nature, that caused us to sin before we were born again, are dead. This is a fact. *Romans 6:6a* says, *"Knowing this, that our old man is crucify with Him."* Paul is not telling us to do something; he is telling us what has already been done. He is stating a fact. But why was this old sinful nature crucified?

Crucifixion with Christ Has a Purpose

The old nature was crucified for this purpose: *"that the body of sin might be destroyed" (Romans 6:6b).* The body of sin refers to the flesh, our sinful patterns of living, our old habits of life, and our old sinful ways of thinking and acting. When Jesus Christ was crucified, your old sinful nature was crucified with Him. At the same time, the body of sin, the flesh, was destroyed.

The word "destroyed" does not mean to annihilate. It means "to render inoperative, to make ineffective." The very moment you asked Jesus Christ to be your Savior , that old sinful nature died and the body of sin was rendered inoperative. It lost its power. It lost its control in your life. At salvation, the rule and the reign of sin were broken. The old sinful habits of life, those entrenched evil patterns of living, lost their power. This means that your body is no longer the servant or slave of sin. It means that you are no longer bound by those old habits and sinful patterns of living. It means that sin is no longer your master and you are no longer sin's slave. The fact is, you have been set free.

Crucifixion with Christ Brings a Result

What is the result of this crucifixion? *Romans 6:6a* says, *"That hence-forth we should not serve sin."* In other words, we are now free not to sin. Do you realize that because of the Lord's death on the cross, sin has no independent authority in your life? Sin does not force you to sin; you sin because you choose to sin. Satan does not make you sin; you sin because you choose to sin.

Not only are you free not to sin, but you are now free to choose God as your new master. Year ago, when I worked for Hyatt

Hotels, I had a boss who was a real taskmaster, a tyrant, a real difficult man to work for. I remember when I first started working for him that he came into my department. Quickly everyone snapped to attention, fear written on every face. He walked straight over to me, looked me square in the eyes, took the soup I had been working on and threw it in the garbage. His actions made me so furious at the time that I felt like picking up my knife and going after him.

Frankly, I didn't know what to expect from day to day. Often he would call me just as my shift was ending and tell me I was to report to another area for several more hours of work. Before I could protest, he would hang up the phone. I had no recourse. On one occasion, he entered my work area and I suppose I said something that upset him. He pushed me against the wall, placed his hand around my throat and picked up a paring knife. I had no idea as to his intention. In my mind I was saying, "It is all over." I was beginning to grieve for my dear wife. He eventually took that knife, cut all the buttons off of the shirt I was wearing, threw the knife down, and stormed out. Well . . . that was my boss.

A wonderful change came into our relationship one day. I walked into his office, presented to him my resignation and said, "I quit." From that moment on our relationship was forever changed. No longer could he intimidate and harass me. No longer could he force me to work long, hard hours. The moment I resigned, he lost all his power, control, and authority in my life.

Several years later, I got a phone call one afternoon. By this time I was pastoring in Singapore. When I picked up the phone and heard that "oh so familiar voice". I felt as though I should leap to attention and salute. Yes, it was he and it was just

When you believed, not only did you receive life in Christ but you also received the power of Christ through the Holy Spirit.

about then I remembered he was no longer my boss and I was no longer his employee. He mentioned that he would be visiting Singapore and would like to have dinner. Before he could suggest the day to meet, I felt like exercising my newfound freedom and authority by saying, "Well, I don't know what day you want to meet for dinner, but I am sure I will be busy." Eventually we did meet and had a wonderful dinner. However, during that entire time, all this former boss could do was to remind me of the authority and power he had once had in my life.

So it is with sin. When you placed your faith in Christ, sin and Satan lost their control and authority in your life and you were free to serve God. The authority of living the victorious Christian life is the cross. Victory begins when we understand that victory is possible.

The Agent Is the Holy Spirit *(v. 2:20b)*

The pathway to victory is nothing more than the Christ-life. It is the life of Christ lived out through our lives. That is exactly what Paul is saying in this verse: *"nevertheless I live; yet not I, but Christ liveth in me."* One of the unique characteristics of Christianity - that which sets it apart from all other religions - is the fact that its Founder lives in the regenerated believer. His influence is not from without, but from within. Just as the sap indwells the branch producing itself in fruit, and just as the blood indwells the body manifesting itself in life, so also Christ indwells the believer reproducing and manifesting His life in him. The agent that makes this life possible is the Holy Spirit. That is the victorious Christian life. It is the indwelling Christ living His life through us. It is the Holy Spirit who makes this possible. He is the agent of victory, and He does two things.

The Holy Spirit Counteracts Sin (Romans 8:2)

In this life we will never be free from the tendency to sin. Even though sin is no longer our master and we are no longer its slave, as long as the presence of sin remains, so does the tendency to sin remain. Not only is it still possible for us to sin, it is at the same time possible for us not to sin. The cross made that possible, and the Holy Spirit makes that actual. In the believer there are two contrasting laws. There is *"the law of sin and death" (Romans 8:2b)*. The law of sin and death refers to the flesh - that old principle and pattern of life. The design of the flesh is to pull you down and recapture and control your life. This law of sin and death is a restless enemy, constantly working to bring you once again under its control. However, there is also in the believer *"the law of the Spirit of life in Christ Jesus" (Romans 8:2a)*. When you believed, not only did you receive life in Christ but you also received the power of Christ through the Holy Spirit. This new law is not there to remove the tendency to sin but to counteract the power of sin. Greater than the downward pull and power of sin is the upward pull and power of the Spirit.

Victory over sin and victory in service comes when we depend upon the Holy Spirit for victory. When we do, His power becomes our power and that power counteracts the power of sin and death. The law of the Spirit of Christ is greater than the law of sin and death. *"Greater is he that is in you, than he that is in the world" (I John 4:4)*. Only when we depend upon the power of the Spirit are we free from the continual downward pull of the flesh.

The law of gravity keeps a plane on the ground. It keeps it from flying. But when a plane reaches a certain speed, another law immediately kicks in and takes over, defying and defeating the law of gravity. This greater law is called the law of aerodynamics. The law of aerodynamics lifts the plane off the ground and keeps it in the air. As long as the law of aerodynamics is in effect, the law of gravity is rendered inoperative. It is just so with the Christian who casts himself in dependence upon the Holy Spirit. The Spirit, which is a greater law, counteracts and defeats the law of sin and death. This counteraction stays in effect as long as one depends upon the Holy Spirit. Many people, for whatever reason, are plagued with nearsightedness. I will call this nearsightedness the law of myopia. Now the law of myopia is easily corrected with a greater law, called the law of corrective lenses. If a person who is afflicted with nearsightedness would apply the law of corrective lenses, the law of myopia would be rendered ineffective, and the poor vision would be corrected. All a person has to do to overcome the law of myopia is to apply the law of corrective lenses. If the law of corrective lenses is constantly applied, then constant victory over the law of myopia is experienced.

So it is with the child of God. There is a greater law available to you; there is a greater law at work in you. There is a law, a power, in you that is greater than the law of sin and death and it is the law of the Spirit of life in Christ. When we apply this law (through utter dependence upon the Holy Spirit), constant victory over the law of sin and death is experienced.

Just as the law of aerodynamics does not eradicate the law of gravity and the law of corrective lenses does not remove the law of myopia, the law of the Spirit of life in Christ does not eradicate sin, nor does it remove the tendency to sin. But the law of the Spirit does counteract the law of sin and death. It renders sin inoperative in the life. *Romans 8:13* says, *"Ye through the Spirit do mortify* [put to death] *the deeds of the body." Galatians 5:16* says *"Walk in the Spirit, and ye shall not fulfill the lust of the flesh."* Victory over sin is found in the counteracting influence of the Holy Spirit. If you depend upon the Spirit, you will not sin. If you continually depend upon the Spirit, you will continually not sin. The Holy Spirit makes practical what the cross made possible. The cross rendered sin inoperable, but the Holy Spirit makes this positional truth practical.

The Holy Spirit Conforms Us to Christ (John 16:14)

When we depend upon the law of the Spirit of life in Christ, not only does the Spirit counteract sin, but He also conforms our lives to Christ. *John 16:14* says, *"He* [the Holy Spirit] *shall glorify Me* [Jesus]." The word *glorify* means "to show, display, manifest, make known." In other words, the function of the Holy Spirit is to make Christ manifest, to display Him. But where is Christ to be made manifest? Where is He to be displayed? He is displayed in and through the believer. The Holy Spirit takes the yielded, surrendered believer and begins to conform his life into the image of Christ. Not only does He conform our lives into the image of Christ, but He also makes Jesus Christ become our very life. His life becomes my life. Christ lives His life out through us. So we begin to live as Jesus lived, walk as Jesus walked, and love as Jesus loved. We begin to possess His peace and His joy and to live His life and experience His power.

II Corinthians 3:18, "But we all, with open face beholding as in a glass the glory of the Lord, are changed into the same image from glory to glory, even as by the Spirit of the Lord." The word translated here as "changed" is the same word translated "transfigured" in *Matthew 17:2*, and *Mark 9:2*, referring to our Lord's transfiguration. By definition, the word means, "to be changed from the inside out." That is what happened to our Lord on the Mount of Transfiguration. There we see Christ's deity shining through His humanity, so in His humanity, His deity is seen. That is what the Holy Spirit does to us. He takes the yielded believer and changes him from the inside out into the same image as Jesus Christ. Thus, in our humanity His deity is seen, His character reflected, and His life experienced. The Holy Spirit begins to conform his life to Christ's life so that he actually lives His life. Paul said, *"I am crucified with Christ: nevertheless I live; yet not I, but Christ liveth in me" (Galatians 2:20).* What Paul is saying is this: "It is not I who lives this life; it is Christ in me." Again Paul says, *"For to me to live is Christ" (Philippians 1:21).*

The victorious life is the Christ-life. When we depend upon the indwelling Spirit, He counteracts sin and conforms us to Christ. His life becomes my life, and His life is lived out through us. Paul says in *Philippians 4:13, "I can do all things through Christ which strengtheneth me."* The phrase through Christ means "in Christ" *or* "in union with Christ." In front of my house is a train track which runs from Singapore to Malaysia. The train consists of a large locomotive or engine. The locomotive can represent Christ with all of His power. Connected to the locomotive is the coach, and this can represent the believer. The coach can go anywhere the locomotive goes and do anything the locomotive does as long as it remains linked to the locomotive, which is the source of its power. As believers we can do anything that Christ may ask; we can walk as He walked, love as He loved, live as He lived. We can have His victory and know His power through the agency of the Holy Spirit. Victory is possible because at the cross sin was rendered inoperative, and through the agency of the Holy Spirit, we are enabled to live in all the fullness of Christ.

The Access Is by Faith *(v. 2:20c)*

The access into the Christ-life is by faith. Paul says, *"the life which I now live in the flesh I live by the faith of the Son of God, who loved me, and gave Himself for me."* Faith appropriates what God provides. What has God provided? Clearly, He has provided victory over sin at the cross and the indwelling Holy Spirit to maintain that victory. Faith lays hold of God's facts and turns them into factors of Christian experience. Faith appropriates what God provides. It claims God's promises. In John's Gospel, the word believe is used some fifty times. In every case, "receive" can be used with equal good sense. To have faith is to believe. To believe is to receive. To receive is to appropriate. To appropriate is to take to one's self as one's own. That is the way to victory-the access is by faith, and faith is simply appropriating what God has provided.

Towering above City Hall in Philadelphia is a statue of William Penn, the Quaker founder of the commonwealth of Pennsylvania. Penn was on very good terms with the Indians, and in recognition of his kindness, they told him that they would give him as much land as he could walk around in one day. He took them at their word. One morning he rose early and walked all day long. When he returned late that night, he was met by a group of Indians with quizzical smiles on their faces. "Pale face has had a long walk today," they said. But they kept their promise, and Penn received all the land, which is now the city of Philadelphia.[1] By faith, he appropriated what the Indians had promised. We are to do the same if we are to find victory. It is not enough to long for victory, or to hope for victory, or even to ask for victory. There is a world of difference between a faith that asks and a faith that appropriates. We need not ask for what God has already provided; we need simply to appropriate, to receive, and to make it our own.

If you have money in the bank, you do not need to plead with the teller to give it to you. All you need do is simply give her a withdrawal slip to receive what is yours. In the same way victory is already yours; you just need to receive it.

The late F. B. Meyer recounted how he learned the secret of appropriation. He was addressing a large gathering of children who became increasingly unruly. He found his patience rapidly coming to an end and knew he was about to lose his temper, over which he never fully reigned. He was ashamed of his failure but was unable to do anything about it. In his extremity, he cried in his heart, "Thy patience, Lord!" Immediately it seemed a lump of the cooling patience of Christ dropped into His heart. All anger and annoyance completely died, and he was able to bring the meeting to a blessed conclusion. The experience was so striking-so decisive-and the

There is a world of difference between a faith that asks and a faith that appropriates. We need not ask for what God has already provided; we need simply to appropriate, to receive, and to make it our own.

deliverance so complete that he knew he had discovered a valuable secret. He testified that afterwards he used the same formula. He retained the words "Thy . . . Lord!" and put between them whatever his present need. When feeling lonely, he would say, "Thy companionship, Lord." When gripped by fear, it was "Thy serenity, Lord." When tempted to impurity, it was "Thy holiness, Lord." And when feeling critical of others, it was "Thy love, Lord." He simply appropriated by faith what God had provided and found victory.[2]

II Peter 1:3 says, *"According as His divine power hath given unto us all things that pertain unto life and godliness"*. Faith appropriates this provision and finds victory. In *II Corinthians 12:9*, Jesus said to Paul, *"My grace is sufficient for thee."* Notice that Jesus did not say, "My grace *might* be sufficient for you." He said, "My grace *is* sufficient for you". All we need is to access this all-sufficient grace through faith.

When you are tempted to sin, appropriate Christ's holiness. When you are tempted to anger, by faith access Christ's peace. When you are tempted to fear, appropriate Christ's fearlessness. When you are tempted to criticize, by faith access Christ's love. When you are mentally not up to the task, appropriate Christ's wisdom. When you feel you cannot do what Christ has called you to do, by faith access Christ's power. Christ's all-sufficient grace is always available - not for the asking, but for the taking - and it is taken by faith. That is the pathway to victory. The authority is the cross; the agent is the Holy Spirit; and the access is by faith.

Our Weakness, God's Weapon

I Corinthians 1:25-2:5

CHAPTER FIVE

Our Weakness, God's Weapon

I Corinthians 1:25-2:5

On Saturday, October 15, 1932, Gladys Aylward left Liverpool station in England bound for China and missionary service. She had no money in her pocket and only the name of a lady who had promised to meet her if she ever reached China. Gladys was born to a poor working-class family. She had little education, no skills, and no particular training. She was not cultured, and with no money to her name, owned nothing. To earn a living, she had worked various jobs as a shop girl, a nanny, and a housemaid.

When God called Miss Aylward to missionary service, she immediately applied to the China Inland Mission but was rejected because "her qualifications were too slight and her education too limited."[1] Although uneducated, theologically untrained, financially bereft, and rejected by men, Gladys Aylward left England for China with nothing but the promises of God. She quickly learned the language simply by listening to it. She began an orphanage and started teaching Bible stories that attracted people from all over the region. In the year 1940, after several years of sowing the Word, Gladys finally saw a great harvest sent by God.

One day as Gladys and a Chinese evangelist were speaking, the building quickly filled to suffocating capacity, and the Holy Spirit came in great power, sweeping multitudes - men, women, and children - into the kingdom of God. God used this uneducated, untrained lady not because she was wise, or mighty, or noble. God used her because she was weak. God did not use her in spite of her obvious human weaknesses; God used her because of her weaknesses. It was because of her weakness that God was able to display His power and do a mighty work.

God's ways are not man's ways. When man is looking for someone to do a great job or to accomplish a great task, he chooses a man of intelligence, wealth, prestige, position. That is not God's way. When God is looking for a man to do a great job or to accomplish a great task, He does not walk the halls of our academic institutions scouring transcripts looking for the best and the brightest of men. He does not wait in the lobbies of our financial institutions or burst into the boardrooms of our largest companies, looking for the richest and wealthiest of men. When God is looking for a man to do a great job, He chooses the foolish to confound the wise and the weak things to confound the mighty. He uses the base and the despised of the world to bring to naught the things that are.

According to God, the greatest man that ever lived-apart from Jesus Christ was John the Baptist. He had no formal education, no training in a trade or profession, no money, no military rank, no political position, no social pedigree, no prestige, no impressive appearance, no gift of oratory. Yet Jesus said, *"Among them that are born of women there hath not risen a greater than John the Baptist" (Matthew 11:11).* In the eyes of the world, John the Baptist was a nobody from nowhere with nothing. That is exactly the reason God used him. God uses nobodies from nowhere with nothing who are willing to depend upon Him for everything.

God Uses Our Weakness (1:26-28)

One of the clearest principles in the Bible is that God uses weak things. He uses men and women who abandon their reliance on their own natural abilities and resources and cast their dependence totally upon God. In *I Corinthians 1:26*, Paul says, *"For ye see your calling, brethren, how that not many wise men after the flesh, not many mighty, not many noble are called."* Notice that Paul did not say that God does not use the wise, the mighty, or the noble. But He does not use "many". God only uses the wise, the mighty, and the noble when they abandon their reliance on their natural abilities and resources and cast their total dependence upon God. In other words, God will not and does not use the gifted, the highly qualified, the intellectual genius, the gifted orator, the financially prosperous, or the multi-talented until he abandons his reliance on those things and depends totally on God. It is only when one is content to be nothing and depend upon nothing but God that God can be everything. It is only when God is everything that God is content to display His

One of the clearest principles in the Bible is that God uses weak things. He uses men and women who abandon their reliance on their own natural abilities and resources and cast their dependence totally upon God.

power. *Isaiah 40:29* says, *"He giveth power* [strength] *to the faint; and to them that have no might he increaseth strength." II Corinthians 3:5* says, *"Not that we are sufficient of ourselves to think any thing as of ourselves; but our sufficiency is of God."* In other words, when we see our own inadequacy, our own inability, our own insufficiency, then we will see God's ability and His sufficiency in every area of our life. *II Corinthians 12:9* says, *"My strength is made perfect in weakness."* The word strength is the word dunamies, from which we get the word dynamite. It is the same word used in *Acts 1:8* translated power. The word perfect is the same word used in *John 19:30* translated finished, meaning "complete." So God's power is made perfect, complete in our weakness. In *II Corinthians 12:10*, Paul says, *"when I am weak, then am I strong."* Our weakness is God's strength. The writer of Hebrews says of those great men and women of faith in *Hebrews 11: 34 "out of weakness [they] were made strong."*

When our Lord was looking for twelve men to carry His message and to advance His kingdom, He did not visit the rabbinical schools, or the theological seminaries, or the leading universities of the day. He did not visit the leading business centers, such as Corinth or Rome. In fact, He passed them by. Instead, He went to the fishing ports, the side streets, and the marketplaces. He went to the common people, and there He chose twelve unschooled, unlettered artisans and fishermen. He chose a group of non-entities, who had nothing, but who were willing to depend upon Him for everything.

It is only when we allow our natural abilities, our talents, our training, and all that we depend upon to fall to the ground and die that we will see God's strength and power. Our weakness is the best backdrop for God to display His power.

D. L. Moody was lacking in education; his physical appearance was often described as unattractive; his voice was high-pitched and nasal. But these weaknesses did not prevent God from using him and shaking the world through him. On one occasion, a press reporter who was assigned to cover Moody's campaigns and discover the secret of his extraordinary power and influence over people of all strata of society wrote, "I can see nothing whatsoever in Moody to account for his marvelous work." Moody, hearing of this, laughed and said, "Of course not, because the work was God's, not mine."[2] Moody's weakness was God's weapon.

Weakness Demands Humility (2:1-4)

Paul had every advantage in life. He was born a Roman citizen, which gave him unique advantages in life. He was a citizen of Tarsus, one of the leading cities of the day. He was born into a wealthy family. He spoke Greek, Hebrew, and Aramaic. He studied Jewish history in Jerusalem under Gamaliel, the leading rabbi of the day. It has been said that he studied philosophy at the University of Tarsus, earning the equivalent of two PhD's. He was skilled with his hands, being a tent maker. Paul was not only educated, wealthy, cultured, and skilled, he was also extremely zealous for his faith. He was a dynamic preacher of the Word and had tireless energy. Humanly speaking, Paul had it all. However, he placed absolutely no confidence in any of these things.

Paul said, *"And I, brethren, when I came to you, came not with excellency of speech or of wisdom, declaring unto you the testimony of God. For I determined not to know any thing among you, save Jesus Christ, and Him crucified. And I was with you in weakness, and in fear, and in much trembling. And my speech and my preaching was not with enticing words of man's wisdom, but in demonstration of the Spirit and power" (II Corinthians 2:1-4).* That is humility. A humble man recognizes his own inability and his own insufficiency and depends upon God alone.

Paul said of himself in *Philippians 3:5-10, "Circumcised the eighth day, of the stock of Israel, of the tribe of Benjamin, an Hebrew of the Hebrews; as touching the law, a Pharisee; concerning zeal, persecuting the church; touching the righteousness which is in the law, blameless. But what things were gain to me, those I counted loss for Christ."* In other words, they meant nothing to Paul. He recognized his own inability and his own insufficiency and cast his dependence upon God. A humble man realizes that *"God resisteth the proud, but giveth grace unto the humble" (James 4:6).* A humble man has a proper evaluation of himself and the older he becomes, the weaker he becomes, or the more honest the evaluation becomes. In *I Corinthians 15:9*, Paul says, *"I am the least of the apostles."* Later in his life he said that he was *"less than the saints."* Then just before his death, he said, *"Christ Jesus came into the world to save sinners; of whom I am chief."* A humble man has a proper evaluation of himself. He realizes that all of his intellect, his training, his experience, and his position in life mean absolutely nothing apart from the supernatural enabling of God.

A humble man has a proper evaluation of himself. He realizes that all of his intellect, his training, his experience, and his position in life mean absolutely nothing apart from the supernatural enabling of God.

If we do not have a proper evaluation of ourselves, then God has a way of bringing us back to reality. God so desires to display His power in us that when we get a little full of ourselves- that is, when we begin to take God's credit, when we start patting ourselves on the back for a job well done- God has a way of setting us straight. In *II Corinthians 12:7*, Paul says about himself, *"Lest I should be exalted above measure . . . there was given to me a thorn in the flesh."* In order to keep Paul humble, weak, and usable, God sent a difficulty. Paul called this difficulty a "thorn." What that thorn was, we do not know. We do know that it was painful, for the word *thorn* means "stake". It was most likely a bodily affliction that was extremely painful. This bodily affliction was with Paul for some fourteen years. But why was the thorn given? And why did God not take it away? We are told in verse 7, *"lest I should be exalted above measure"* lest he lose his humility and his weakness and thus lose God's power.

God often brings infirmities, difficulties, sicknesses, and various types of suffering into our lives in order to humble us and to keep us dependent upon Him so that He can display His power and use us in the lives of others. Jacob became a prince, having power with men and God, only after God touched his thigh and withered his strength. God made him weak so that he could be made strong.

Humility Brings Dependence (2:1-4)

God requires humility to keep us weak. We are to be weak so that we are left with no choice but to depend upon God. Our problem today is not our weakness but our strength. We live in a day where everything is available to us. We can receive the best training and the best education. We can learn to play a variety of musical instruments. We can be trained to be poised and polished before people. We can be trained to preach and teach well. We can learn to manage and make lots of money or to lead and organize a Fortune 500 company. We can learn to analyze and fix the most complicated of problems. Although these things are good, they can actually be a hindrance and rob us of our usability. When a person thinks that because of all his training, talents, and learned or natural abilities that God must use him, he is deceived and sadly misled. The fact is that God uses those who are dependent upon nothing but Him alone. God humbles us to make us dependent on Him so that He can use us for His glory.

Moses, like Paul, had every advantage in life. He had a royal upbringing. He was raised in Pharaoh's court. He received the best education of the day. He was cultured, refined, extremely proud, and self-sufficient. When Moses saw an Egyptian abusing his fellow countryman, Moses, that self-proclaimed deliverer, attempted single-handedly to deliver his countryman. But Moses failed. For Moses was not ready to be Israel's deliverer. In order to prepare him, God banished Moses from Egypt and enrolled him in a forty-year course on weakness, humility, and dependence in preparation for greater service. Moses thoroughly mastered the difficult lessons on weakness, humility, and dependence. For when God called Moses to deliver Israel, Moses shrank from the task. Moses gave God seven reasons that he could not do what God had called him to do. Moses said. "Who am I? What will I say? I lack a message" *(Exodus 3:11)*. "I lack authority" *(3:13)*. "I lack eloquence" *(4:10)*. "I lack special adaptation" *(4:13)*. "I lack previous success" *(5:23)*. "I lack previous acceptance" *(6:12)*. In other words, Moses was saying, "But God I am not able; I am not qualified; I am not capable; I am not trained for this. This is beyond me, get someone else." These excuses made God angry, for Moses' inability was the very reason God had chosen him for the task. Moses was now ready to deliver Israel. He just did not know it. He had learned his lessons of weakness, humility, and dependence well. Moses was now emptied of his self-confidence and his self-dependency, and he was now ready to depend totally on God. His weakness would become God's weapon.

He has to first remove our strength and bring us to the end of ourselves so that we will look at the task and say, "God, I cannot do this without Your strength."

That is how God works. He has to first remove our strength and bring us to the end of ourselves so that we will look at the task and say, "God, I cannot do this without Your strength."

When God called Gideon to deliver the nation of Israel, Gideon said, *"O my Lord, wherewith shall I save Israel? Behold, my family is poor in Manasseh, and I am the least in my father's house" (Judges 6:15).* After God encouraged Gideon that the victory was certain, God put Gideon to the test. When all the troops rallied for battle, there were 32,000 Israelites and 135,000 Midianites. Israel was greatly outnumbered, but God thought Israel was too strong. So He weakened Israel by sending 22,000 home. Now there were 10,000 Israelites and 135,000 Midianites. Still, God thought Israel was too strong. So He weakened them further and sent another 9,700 men home. With only 300 men against Midian's 135,000, Israel was outnumbered 450-1. Yet God thought they were still too strong. So, He weakened them even further. Instead of providing weapons such as bows and arrows, swords, spears, or shields, God gave them fragile pitchers, flaming torches, and rude trumpets. Now Israel, tragically outnumbered and outgunned, was ready for the battle. In this state of absolute weakness, God displayed His power and brought Israel the victory.

That is how God works. The utter weakness of Gideon and his small band of men was God's weapon for victory. God stripped Gideon of all human resources so that he had no choice but to depend on God. God uses weak things. Weakness demands humility, and humility brings dependence. When God strips us, breaks us, and brings us to the end of ourselves, then we will depend upon Him alone. And only when we are depending on Him will He display His power.

Dependence Displays God's Power (1:27-28)

How is it that the foolish things of the world are able to confound the wise? How is it that the weak things of the world are able to confound the things that are mighty? How is it that the base and despised things of the world are able to bring to naught the things that are? *(1:27-28)* The Scripture says that the foolish, the weak, the base, and the despised depend on God, and God is pleased to display His power.

God displays His power in the foolish, the weak, the base, and the despised to show the world that it is not the work of man but unmistakably the work of God *(II Corinthians 1:29)*. If people can explain what we do and how we live apart from the supernatural enabling of God, then we are not yet weak enough. We are not yet broken enough. We are not yet dependent enough. Our weakness is God's weapon that displays God's power, letting the world know that God is at work.

In the last week of July and the first week of August 2001, I took a group to the city of Malaybalay on the island of Mindanao in the Philippines to be trainers for a week of soulwinning training. Our trainees were twenty-five pastors and full-time workers. These men were rugged mountain preachers, pioneers, trailblazers, and self-supporting church planters. Many were leaders, overseeing large works, and most had ten to fifteen years of experience. Our trainers were nobodies from nowhere with nothing. They were two businessmen and eight ladies. Several of the ladies were housewives, and two were single. One was a pastor's wife, and the others were working professionals. One of the ladies had been saved only a year. None of the people had any theological training, and all had very little soulwinning experience. Most had been trained within six months of the trip. From the start, we were disadvantaged. We did not know the people or the place. It was a different culture, and we were limited by language.

When these rugged, experienced warriors of the faith saw that they were to be trained by a group of inexperienced lay people, made up of mostly women, they were surprised. Some were aghast with indignation. Others succumbed to pride, saying, "What can they teach us? What can we learn from them? How are these English speakers going to reach our people?" The team was also intimidated. These inexperienced trainers were not comfortable training these experienced warriors of the faith. One of our ladies came to me before the training session and said, "You must change my trainees; I cannot do this." She had in her group the pastor of the host church, which also happened to be the largest church in the region, and his key deacon. I reminded her that "God uses weak things.".

From the first day God blessed, and within five days over 450 people had been saved. These nobodies from nowhere with nothing, who were willing to depend upon God for everything, took the gospel to the park, the state college, the hospital, the school dormitories, and the boarding houses, and through their weakness God displayed His power. At the end of the week, pastor after pastor testified with a tear in his eye, thanking God for bringing his trainer and displaying His power through his or her weakness. Three pastors testified that they had determined to resign from their ministries at the end of the year, and they would have, had God not displayed His power through these weak vessels. God uses weak things, and weakness demands humility. Humility brings dependence, and dependence displays God's power. Our weakness is God's weapon.

What is the Holy Spirit to You?

II Corinthians 13:14

CHAPTER SIX

What is the Holy Spirit to You?

II Corinthians 13:14

For seventeen years, Dr. Walter Wilson was engaged in Bible study and Christian service, but his efforts were fruitless. This barrenness of ministry caused him great sorrow and regret. One day in 1913, a French missionary, who was visiting Dr. Wilson's home, asked him this question, "What is the Holy Spirit to you?" Dr. Wilson replied, "One of the Persons of the God-head." The missionary then said, "Dr. Wilson, you have not answered my question. What is the Holy Spirit to you? What does He mean to you?" Dr. Wilson thought for a moment and then said, "He is nothing to me. I know who He is, but I have no personal relationship with him!" The missionary then replied, "This is the reason for the barrenness and fruitlessness of your ministry."[1]

I was once asked this very same question. I had just graduated from Bible College and was sitting before an ordination council of some ten men, all of whom were pastors or professors. They were checking my theology, asking me nearly every question under the sun. Near the end of the session, my pastor, who was a godly man, asked me, "What do you know about the ministry of the Holy Spirit?" So for a few minutes, I waxed eloquent about the Holy Spirit being God, His omnipotence, omnipresence, omniscience, and so on. My pastor stopped me and said, "No, that is not what I am asking. What do you know of the Holy Spirit and His power in your life, work, and ministry?" I was stunned. My jaw dropped to the ground, and my tongue began to stutter and stammer. I was left blank with no real concrete answer. I knew about Him, but I had no personal relationship with Him.

I would venture to say that if we were to ask others the same question, we would likely get a variety of answers. To most Christians, the Holy Spirit is but a doctrine, a theology, the third person of the Godhead, but nothing more. To others, the Holy Spirit is a mysterious unknown power that they try unsuccessfully to get hold of and use. To some, He is a servant whom they can call upon when in need. But the question that each of us must consider is "What is the Holy Spirit to you?"

He Is a Divine Person

One reason the Holy Spirit is nothing to so many is because He is seen and treated as a mere influence, a power emanating from God. He is often seen and treated as an impersonal "it." One thing is absolutely certain in the Bible; the Holy Spirit is divine. In *Matthew 28:19*, the Holy Spirit is recognized as one of the Persons of the Trinity, on even par with God the Father and God the Son. In *Hebrews 9:14*, the Holy Spirit is called "the Eternal Spirit." In *Acts 5:3-4*, the

One reason the Holy Spirit is nothing to so many is because He is seen and treated as a mere influence, a power emanating from God.

Holy Spirit is called "God," and in *Job 33:4* and *John 6:63*, the Spirit is seen as the member of the Godhead who gives life to men. The Holy Spirit is divine; He is God.

He is not a force or an influence; neither is He an impersonal "it." The Spirit is a Divine Person. Jesus in *John 14-16* gave the greatest discourse on the Holy Spirit. Twelve times the Lord mentions the Holy Spirit and not once does He describe Him as an influence, a mere power, or an impersonal "it." Jesus said, *"Howbeit when He* [not it], *the Spirit of truth, is come He* [not it] *will guide you into all truth: for He* [not it] *shall not speak of Himself; but whatsoever He* [not it] *shall hear, that shall He* [not it] *speak: and He* [not it] *will show you things to come" (John 16:13).* The Holy Spirit is not a mere power emanating from God. He is not an impersonal "it." He is a Divine Person who loves, guides, cares, corrects, comforts, councils, enables and empowers.

Not long ago a pastor was preaching on the person of the Holy Spirit. After the sermon, a lady came up to him and began to reprove him for the exalted position he had given the Holy Spirit. As she talked, the lady kept referring to the Holy Spirit as "it." The preacher listened carefully to see whether she knew the Holy Spirit as a Person and whether she loved Him as a member of the Trinity. When it was evident that she did not, the pastor asked, "May I have an imaginary conversation with Mrs. Price who lives down the street?" The lady gave her permission, and the pastor began his imaginary conversation. He said, "Mrs. Price, I am happy to tell you that Mrs. Schwartz came to the conference. It came all week. I asked it if it was saved, and it said yes." Mrs. Schwartz interrupted the pastor saying, "Why are you calling me 'it'?" The pastor said, "Please, Mrs. Schwartz, do not interrupt my story." Then he continued. "I asked it to tell me how it got saved. It replied, 'I believed it died for me at Calvary and bore my sins by shedding its blood on the cross.' " By this time, Mrs. Schwartz was offended and exclaimed, "That is blasphemy! How can you refer to the Lord as an 'it'! And why are you doing it?" The preacher replied, "During our entire conversation, you referred to the Holy Spirit as an 'it'." Her expression changed, and in fear, she said, "O God, please forgive me for insulting the Spirit as I have done." Then she said to the pastor, "I clearly see that the Holy Spirit has never been to me a real Person. But here and now, I acknowledge Him as my God, my Lord, and God's gift to me."[2] The Holy Spirit is a Divine Person. As a Divine Person, He is to be thanked, trusted, and talked with.

He Is to Be Talked With

The Holy Spirit is to be communicated with. He is to be prayed to. In *Matthew 9:37-38*, Jesus said, *"The harvest truly is plenteous, but the labourers are few; pray ye therefore the Lord of the harvest, that He will send forth labourers."* The Lord of the harvest is the Holy Spirit. It is the Holy Spirit who leads men and women into service and into the harvest fields where there are people who need to be saved. It was the Holy Spirit who led Philip to the Ethiopian eunuch in *Acts 8*. It was the Holy Spirit who said, *"Separate me Barnabas and Saul for the work whereunto I have called them" (Acts 13).* It was the Holy Spirit who led Paul to Troas where he heard the Macedonian call, *"Come over and help us" (Acts 16).* It was the Holy Spirit who led Paul to Philippi and then to Lydia, who was saved along with her household *(Acts 16).* The Holy Spirit is the Lord of the harvest, and we are to talk with Him about the harvest. We are to ask Him to lead us to people who need to be saved. We are to ask Him to convict and convince men of sin, righteousness, and God's coming judgment *(John 16:8).* We are to ask the Holy Spirit to save and regenerate the lost. We are to ask Him to teach us and to give us the words that we are to speak when we need them.

In *John 14:16*, Jesus said, *"And I will pray to the Father, and He shall give you another Comforter, that He may abide with you forever."* The word another means "another of the exact same kind." Jesus promised that when the Holy Spirit came, The Spirit would stand in His place. He would be to the disciples then what Christ was to them now. Just as the disciples communicated with the Lord, we are to communicate with the Spirit. Just as the disciples asked the Lord to teach them to pray, we are now to ask the Holy Spirit to be our Divine Teacher.

Some may object to this based on *John 16:13*, but the verse does not say that we cannot speak to the Spirit. It says, *"He shall not speak of* [or from] *Himself."* What the Lord is saying in context is that the Holy Spirit will not speak anything that is different from what Christ taught. In the Bible we are never forbidden to talk with, communicate with, or pray to the Holy Spirit. It stands to reason that this Divine Person, who is co-equal with God the Father and God the Son, should be communicated with and talked to. We are to talk with Him as we talk with the other two members of the Trinity. If you are not talking with the Holy Spirit about the harvest, then "What is the Holy Spirit to you?"

He Is to Be Thanked

We are to thank Him, praise Him, and give Him credit for what He has done and what He is continuing to do in our lives and in the lives of others. If the Holy Spirit has led you to go somewhere or to do something or to say something, you should give Him the credit and thank Him for it. If the Holy Spirit has taught you a wonderful truth from God's Word, you should thank Him for doing so. If the Holy Spirit has used you in the life of an individual, you should thank Him for using you. If the Holy Spirit has brought to your heart comfort, you should thank Him for that comfort.

Micah gave the Holy Spirit credit for the power he received in service *(Micah 3:8)*. Paul gave the Holy Spirit credit for empowering his witness *(Acts 20:23)*. Paul gave the Holy Spirit credit for being the One who hindered him from staying in Bythyania and Galatia. He also gave the Spirit credit for being the One who led him to Macedonia *(Acts 16:6-10)*. Agabus gave the Holy Spirit credit for being the One who warned Paul of coming danger *(Acts 21:11)*.

We must begin treating the Holy Spirit as a Divine Person. We often honor God the Father and God the Son, but when was the last time you honored, thanked, or praised God the Holy Spirit for what He has done and what He is doing daily in your life? To ask the Holy Spirit to do something and then to never thank or praise Him for it is to insult Him. It is flat-out rude.

Say, for example, you were riding in my car on a very wet and rainy day. All of a sudden, one of the tires goes flat, and I ask you, "Please get out and fix the tire." So you step out into the wind, the mud, and the rain, and you fix the tire. When you get back into the car, I do not say anything to you. After awhile I might say, "Watch your muddy feet," or I might say, "Do not get my nice car all wet." But I never say, "Thank you." I never say, "Thank you for getting all wet and muddy for me." How would you feel? Let me ask you, "Would that be a nice thing to do?" Likely none of us would be so rude to our friends, but we do it all the time to this Divine Person called the Holy Spirit. If you are not thanking the Holy Spirit for what He does and for what He is doing in your life or in the lives of others, then "What is the Holy Spirit to you?"

He Is to Be Trusted

We can trust the Holy Spirit to teach us and to lead us to the people who need to be saved. We can trust Him to give us wisdom to make the right choices and the right decisions in life. We can trust the Holy Spirit to give us the words to say and to bring the right Bible verses to our minds when we need them. We can trust the Holy Spirit to give us victory over sin and power in service. We can trust the Holy Spirit in the lives of others. We can trust Him to raise up new leadership. We can trust Him to guide our leadership. One reason our ministries and people spiritually "limp along" is that we do not trust the Spirit of God to work in them. We are control freaks. We must control everything and everybody. As a result, we hinder the work of the Holy Spirit and stifle what He would like to do. We do not trust the Spirit to lead our leaders. We do not trust the Holy Spirit to control our services and our prayers meetings, thus we oftentimes rob them of life. We must to trust the Holy Spirit.

The early church trusted the Holy Spirit in the selection of elders for the church in Ephesus *(Acts 20:28)*. Peter trusted the Holy Spirit to open the hearts of the Gentiles *(Acts 11:12)*. Paul trusted the Holy Spirit to make him holy and to maintain his godliness *(Romans 8:5)*. Peter depended upon the Holy Spirit for power in preaching *(I Peter 1:12)*. We must trust this Divine Person in the same way.

In our church in Singapore, I had just preached on the Holy Spirit being a Divine Person who can be talked to, thanked, and trusted. One of our young ladies took the message to heart and decided to put the truth to the test. A group had met early that morning for prayer, and afterwards she asked the Holy Spirit to lead her into the harvest and to take her to a soul that needed to be saved. Not long after that prayer to the Holy Spirit, she was walking through an outdoor food court when she caught the eye of a young lady. This young lady was a Malay and obviously Islamic by religion. The church sister hesitated and thought to herself, "Surely this is not the person. She is Malay and Islamic." But she said, "Lord, if you want me to witness to this person, then when I turn back, have her look at me and smile." When she turned back, the young lady was looking right at her, eye-to-eye, and gave her a big smile. So she trusted the prompting of the Holy Spirit and sat down with her. The Lord of the harvest opened the door and the heart of this young Islamic lady and she was wonderfully saved. The young lady said, "Although I was from an Islamic home, I had wanted to become a Christian for over four years, but no one ever told me how until now." The Holy Spirit is a Divine Person who can be talked with, thanked, and trusted. If you are not talking to, thanking, and trusting this Divine Person, then "What is the Holy Spirit to you?"

He Is a Dynamic Power

This Divine Person is also a Person of Dynamic Power. The Holy Spirit is a Power equal to the Power of the Father and the Power of the Son. It was the Holy Spirit who brooded over the waters of the deep, assisting God the Father in the creation of the world *(Psalm 33:6)*. It was the Holy Spirit who imparted life to this lump of clay and made it a living being *(Job 33:4)*. It was the Holy Spirit, who over a span of sixteen hundred years, took forty men from various backgrounds (farmers, fishermen, shepherds, servants, teachers, and tax collectors), from various places (from the caves of Adul-lum to the wilderness of Judea, from the prisons of Rome to the palaces of Zion), speaking different languages (Hebrew, Aramaic, and Greek) and guided them to write exactly what He wanted without violating their personalities, vocabulary, or style and without robbing them of their opinions, thoughts, and fears. These men from different backgrounds and various periods of time produced a book of perfect unity, without contradictions - a book called the Bible. This book is His inspiration *(II Peter 1:21)*. It was the Holy Spirit who placed the seed in Mary's womb, who produced the Son of God wrapped in human flesh. It was the Spirit who enabled Christ to be victorious over the subtle slander of Satan in the wilderness *(Luke 4:1)*. It was the Spirit who enabled Christ to heal the sick, loosen the tongue of the dumb, and deliver the people from demons *(Matthew 12:28)*. It was the Holy Spirit who enabled Christ to wipe the drops of blood from His brow in the Garden and to willingly go the cross *(Hebrews 9:14)*. It was the Holy Spirit who quickened Christ's lifeless body and raised Him from the grave *(Romans 8:11)*. It is the Holy Spirit who regenerates the spiritually dead and makes them spiritually alive *(John 3:5-6)*. It is the Holy Spirit who puts to death the deeds of the body and fights the flesh *(Galatians 5:16; Romans 8:13)*. And it is the Holy Spirit who illumines His inspiration, transforming us into the image of Christ *(II Corinthians 3:18)*. The Holy Spirit is a Divine Person of Dynamic Power.

This Divine Person of Dynamic Power lives in you. *I Corinthians 3:16* says, *"Know ye not that ye are the temple of God, and that the spirit of God dwelleth in you?" I Corinthians 6:19* says, *"Know ye not that your body is the temple of the Holy Ghost, which is in you?"* Dwelling within you is this Divine Person of Dynamic Power. If this Divine Person of Dynamic Power dwells in you, His presence should make a difference.

If this Divine Person of Dynamic Power dwells in you, then His presence should make a difference.

He Should Make a Difference in Your Personal Life

When we understand that dwelling within us is God the Holy Spirit, this reality should make a difference in our lives. Instead of grumbling, complaining, arguing, and worrying, we should have peace, joy, and contentment. There should be a song in the soul and thanksgiving on the tongue.

He Should Make a Difference in Your Domestic Life

The Holy Spirit will enable a wife to submit to her husband, the husband to love his wife, and the children to obey their parents. It is the indwelling Spirit who will enable the parents to rear their children in the nurture and admonition of the Lord. It is the Holy Spirit's desire that we have happy, harmonious, and healthy homes. They ought to be little heavens on earth. Instead of happy, harmonious little heavens on earth, many homes are filled with little monsters that produce hopeless headaches. Often our homes seem more like "hell" than heaven. What we have forgotten is that dwelling in each of us is this Person of Power who desires to lead, guide, and enable us to be the person He wants us to be. What we have forgotten is that in each child of God is the Holy Spirit, who can give us the love we need to bind hearts together.

He Should Make a Difference in Our Business Life

This indwelling Spirit will give both employee and employer the wisdom to meet the challenges of each and every day. The Holy Spirit should be making a difference in your life. If He is not, maybe it is because you have not made this Divine Person of Dynamic Power your Daily Partner.

He Is a Daily Partner

In *II Corinthians 13:14*, we are told, *"The grace of the Lord Jesus Christ, the love of God, and the communion of the Holy Ghost, be with you all."* The word communion (*kononia*) means "fellowship, sharer, or companion." The best word to sum up what this word means is the word partner. The Holy Spirit is to be our partner. Four times in *John 14-16*, Jesus calls the Holy Spirit our comforter (*parakletos*), meaning "one called alongside of to give aid." When these two words are brought together, we are given a beautiful picture of the Holy Spirit and His relationship to us. He is a Divine Person of Dynamic Power called alongside as our Daily Partner to enable our walk and empower our work and witness. If the Holy Spirit is going to be our Daily Partner, enabling our walk and empowering our work and witness, we must yield ourselves to Him as both Lord and Leader of our lives.

He Must Be Lord and Leader of Your Life

The Holy Spirit will only be free to do His work in our lives when we hand ourselves over to Him as Lord and Leader of our lives. *Romans 12:1* says, *"I beseech you*

He is a Divine Person of Dynamic Power called alongside as our Daily Partner to enable our walk and empower our work and witness.

therefore, brethren, by the mercies of God, that ye present your bodies a living sacrifice, holy, and acceptable unto God, which is your reasonable service." If the Holy Spirit is going to be Lord and Leader, we must present our bodies to Him.

Paul says, *"Know ye not that your body is the temple of the Holy Ghost" (I Corinthians 6:19).* We are to present this body, this temple, to the indwelling Holy Spirit that He might control our life as Lord and Leader. It is only when this is done that He can enable our walk and empower our witness. It is only when He is Lord that our feet are free to go where He wants them to go. It is only when He is Lord that our lips will speak His message. It is only when He is Lord that we can see what He wants us to see. It is only when He is Lord that our minds will think what He wants us to think. It is only when He is Lord that our hearts will love the way He wants us to love.

Lordship Is the Spirit Using You - Not You Using the Spirit

Lordship is not asking the Holy Spirit to be our helper. When you ask someone to help you to do a bit of work, you remain the master and the helper is only the servant. If someone helps you clean your home or wash your car or file your letters, that one is your servant doing as you command. For years I worked as a chef in hotels all over the United States. As a chef, I had lots of helpers. They were called cooks. The cooks assisted the chef. When I needed something or wanted something done, I called one of the cooks to do it. I was the boss, and they did what I wanted done. I did not do what they wanted done. They helped me. I was not helping them. The Holy Spirit is not my helper. He is not one of my cooks that I can call upon whenever I need something done. The Holy Spirit does not operate that way. He demands total control and complete leadership of the life. He is the Chef. He is to be in charge, and we are to be His helpers, doing His work as He commands. Lordship is not the Spirit doing my work and my will but rather it is me doing the Spirit's work and His will. It is not the believer using the Spirit of God, but rather the Spirit of God using the believer. When we see the Spirit as our helper to accomplish our will rather than our being His vessel used by Him to accomplish His will, we rob ourselves of His partnership and His power.

In 1921, Douglas Brown (pastor of the Ramsden Road Baptist Church in London, England) surrendered to the Lordship and Leadership of the Holy Spirit. For months, the Holy Spirit had been calling Mr. Brown to evangelism, but he had resisted because he "did not want to plead with men." When he finally surrendered to the Lordship and Leadership of the Holy Spirit, Douglas Brown resigned from his church and went to Lowstoft, a fishing village in southern England, to hold a series of evangelistic meetings. From the opening night, the Spirit of God moved in a remarkable way and hundreds were saved. This began a moving of the Spirit that swept through all of southern England and East Anglia bringing thousands into the kingdom of God. This moving of the Spirit is classified as England's last revival. From 1921 to mid-1922 Douglas Brown preached 1,700 times. So powerful was the ministry of the Holy Spirit through him that a committee of men, wanting to spread the revival to other cities, began organizing his meetings and choosing which cities and churches in which he would speak. No longer was Douglas Brown free to be led by the Holy Spirit. Not long after this Brown said to a group of preachers, "Pray for me; I have lost my power."[3] As quickly as the revival had started, it stopped. Somehow they forgot that Lordship is the Holy Spirit using you, not you using Him.

Lordship Is Active Cooperation - Not Idle Passivity

Lordship is not sitting back doing nothing, waiting for a sign or some word *from* God before doing anything *for* God. God works in cooperation with man *(Colossians 1:29)*. God works "through us," not "instead of us". Lordship is making our whole being available for His use. It is like driving a car. I do not get into the car, turn the engine on, begin driving, and then say, "All right, Holy Spirit, you can have complete control of my life." So I take my hands off the steering wheel, foot off the gas pedal, and say, "I am yours. Take control!" No. Instead, I do the driving, and the Holy Spirit does the directing. I sit in the driver's seat, turn the car on, and begin driving, but along the way the Holy Spirit, who is sitting in the passenger seat, says, "Turn right." Since He is the Lord and Leader of my life, I do what He says and turn right. Then He says, "Turn left," and since He is Lord and Leader, I turn left. Then He says, "Stop," and since He is Lord and Leader, I do what He says. Lordship is not idle passivity. It is not sitting back doing nothing like a jellyfish floating on the warm currents of the Gulf Stream. It is not me taking my hands off the steering wheel of my life. It is following the Spirit's leadership. And to follow His leadership, we must exchange the leadership of our lives for His leadership. It is making my whole being available for His use.

Lordship Is the Spirit Getting More of You - Not You Getting More of The Spirit.

If we think of the Holy Spirit as merely a power of influence our constant thought will be "How can I get more of Him?" However, if we see Him as a Divine Person of Dynamic Power who desires to be our Daily Partner, our thought will be "How can the Holy Spirit have more of me?" Lordship is not you getting more of Him; rather it is you allowing the Holy Spirit to get more of you. When the Holy Spirit is Lord and Leader of your life, this Divine Person of Dynamic Power will be your Daily Partner, enabling your walk and empowering your work and witness. Have you made the Holy Spirit the Lord and Leader or your life?

One year after Dr. Walter Wilson was asked the question, "What is the Holy Spirit to you?" he heard a sermon preached by James M. Grey from *Romans 12:1.* At the conclusion of his message, Grey leaned over the pulpit and said, "Have you noticed this verse does not tell us *whom* we are to give our bodies to? It is not the Lord Jesus; He has His own body. It is not the Father; He remains on the throne. But it is the Holy Spirit to whom you are to give your body. Your body is the temple of the Holy Spirit and you are requested in that passage to give it to Him for His possession. Will you do this tonight?" Dr. Wilson left the service deeply impressed with the thought that this was the answer to his deepest need and the barren fruitlessness of his life. Upon arriving home, he laid himself on the floor and opened his Bible to *Romans 12:1.* Placing his finger on the text, he said, "Never before have I come to You with myself; I do so now. You may have my body, my feet, my lips, my brain, my hands-all that I have is Yours. My body is Yours to live in and to do with as You please. Just now I make You my Lord, and I receive You as my personal God." The next morning he said to his wife, "This will be a wonderful day. Last night, I received the Holy Spirit into my life as both Lord and Leader and I know He will use me." His wife encouraged him to let her know if anything unusual happened that day. At 11:00 A.M., two young ladies came into Dr. Wilson's office. They were sisters selling advertising. The Spirit of God spoke through Dr. Wilson's lips, and both sisters were wonderfully saved. That was the beginning of a life of evangelistic fruitfulness. Dr. Wilson eventually founded a church, a Bible college, and a mission board. He said, "The change that took place that day (December 21, 1914) was greater than the change that took place when I was saved."[4]

Have you made the Holy Spirit your Lord and Leader? If not, then "What is the Holy Spirit to you?".

CHAPTER seven

The Priority of the Spirit's Power

Acts 1:8

CHAPTER SEVEN

The Priority of the Spirit's Power

Acts 1:8

Christianity is filled with forgotten heroes–men and women used mightily of God but whose names and ministries for some reason have been lost. One such forgotten hero is a man name Jock Troup. Jock was born in Scotland in 1896. He was converted in 1919 while serving in the navy. Soon after his conversion Jock became burdened for the souls of his fellow fishermen. He would work from 6:00 am to 6:00 pm as a fisherman. After work, he would spend hours working as a "fisher of men." Wherever men and women gathered, whether in the marketplace or the village square, Jock would be pleading for their souls. So bold was his witness and so powerful was his preaching that thousands would gather to hear this unlearned fisherman preach the gospel. In a typical fishing village of 2,000 people, Jock would stand in the market square to preach and over 3,000 people would gather to listen. In one such village with 1,500 people, over one~third~600 souls–were converted to Christ in two weeks. Everywhere Jock went and every time he preached, hundreds would be saved. So great was the conviction of sin that often strong men fell to the ground weeping and pleading to God for mercy.

For thirty-four years, God used this unlearned, uncultured fisherman to reach people from both the working and wealthy classes of Scotland and England. He won untold thousands to the Lord. What was the secret of his ministry? Why did God use this humble man? The answer is this: "In 1920 at the Fisherman's Mission in Aberdeen, Scotland, Jock Troup entered into a definite experience with the Holy Spirit."[1] In other words, he was filled with the Spirit and empowered for service. In biblical terms, he entered into the reality of *Acts 1:8*, which says, *"But ye shall receive power, after that the Holy Ghost is come upon you: and ye shall be witnesses unto me."*

As children of God, our greatest need today is to know the power of the Holy Spirit. In your Bible, like mine, the book of Acts is entitled "The Acts of the Apostles." This I believe to be not only inaccurate but also an inappropriate title for the book. The book of Acts is not so much the acts of the apostles as it is the acts of the Holy Spirit *through* the apostles. Everything the apostles did in the book of Acts, was done in the power of the Holy Spirit. They preached the Word in the power of the Holy Spirit. They witnessed in the power of the Holy Spirit. They administered the church in the power of the Holy Spirit. They were led to begin new ministries by the power of the Holy Spirit. They endured opposition by the power of the Holy Spirit. Any and all spiritual success experienced was the direct result of the Holy Spirit's power.

If we are going to impact our world for Jesus Christ, if our preaching, teaching, and witnessing is going to make a difference, if we are going to live above the status quo, if we are going to expect any measure of victory, then we must have the power of the Holy Spirit on our lives, work, and ministries. If we are going to know His power, we must see the Spirit's power as priority.

The Example of Christ

It is sobering to realize that Jesus did not begin His public ministry until He was filled with the Holy Spirit and power. In *Luke 3:21-22*, we are told that after Jesus had been baptized and was praying, *"The heaven was opened, and the Holy Ghost descended in a bodily shape like a dove upon Him."* The next thing we read, with nothing intervening but the human genealogy of Jesus, is *"And Jesus being full of the Holy Ghost returned from Jordan, and was led by the Spirit into the wilderness" (Luke 4:1).* Then from the wilderness temptation, *"Jesus returned in the power of the Spirit into Galilee: and there went out a fame of Him through all the region round about. And He taught in their synagogues, begin glorified of all" (Luke 4:14-15).* From the synagogue in Galilee, Jesus went to the synagogue in Nazareth, where He read from *Isaiah 61:1* saying, *"The Spirit of the Lord is upon Me, because He hath anointed Me to preach the gospel to the poor; He hath sent me to heal the brokenhearted, to preach deliverance to the captives, and recovering of sight to the blind, to set at liberty them that are bruised. To preach the acceptable year of the Lord" (Luke 4:18).* Jesus did not begin His earthly ministry until He was filled with the Spirit-setting us an example that

Jesus did not begin His earthly ministry until He was filled with the Spirit-setting us an example that we should follow in His steps and reminding us of the absolute necessity of living a Spirit-filled life.

we should follow in His steps and reminding us of the absolute necessity of living a Spirit–filled life.

It is also sobering to realize that everything Jesus did in His earthly ministry–all the good He did, all the healings He performed, and all the oppressed He delivered - He did in the power of the Holy Spirit. Jesus taught in the power of the Holy Spirit *(Luke 4:32)*. He cast out devils in the power of the Holy Spirit *(Luke 4:36)*. He was led by the Holy Spirit *(Luke 4:1)*. He rejoiced in the power of the Holy Spirit *(Luke 10:21)*. He went to the cross by the power of the Holy Spirit *(Hebrews 9:14)*. Peter sums up our Lord's life with these words: *"How God anointed Jesus of Nazareth with the Holy Ghost and with power: who went about doing good, and healing all that were oppressed of the devil; for God was with Him" (Acts 10:38)*. If Jesus Christ who is God and yet truly human did not begin His earthly ministry until He was empowered by the Spirit, if Jesus did all He did in His earthly ministry in the power of the Holy Spirit, how much more should we?

The Experience of the Disciples

It is also sobering to realize that the disciples could not begin their public ministry, nor could they begin the task of reaching the world, until they were filled with the Spirit and empowered for service. The Lord said to these disciples in *Acts 1:4: "And, being assembled together with them, commanded them that they should not depart from Jerusalem, but wait for the promise of the Father."* These men were commanded to wait. Yet, from a human perspective, they had everything.

They were saved men. In *John 15:3*, Jesus referring to the eleven disciples, for Judas had already departed, said, *"Now ye are clean through the word which I have spoken unto you."*

They were experienced men. For three and a half years they had traveled with the Lord. Obviously, they knew the ropes. They knew what it was to evangelize and to witness and how to draw a crowd, for they often traveled with the Lord on His evangelistic tours *(Matthew 9:35-38)*.

They were educated men. Three and a half years had found them sitting at the Master's feet. And for forty days between the Lord's resurrection and His ascension, they attended a crash course on things pertaining to the kingdom of God *(Acts 1:3)*.

They were Spirit-indwelt men. In *John 20:22*, Jesus breathed on them and said, *"Receive ye the Holy Ghost."* This was neither a symbolic nor a prophetic breathing, but at that very moment they received the Holy Spirit as a permanent indwelling. In *John 7:37-39*, Jesus said, *"If any man thirst, let him come unto Me, and drink. He that believeth on Me, as the scripture hath said, out of his belly shall flow rivers of living water. (But this spake He of the Spirit, which they that believe on Him should receive: for the Holy Ghost was not yet given; because that Jesus was not yet glorified.)"* The word "glorified" is a word unique to John and in context refers to Christ's death *(cf. 11:4; 12:16, 23; 13:31)*. So, any time after Christ's death, the Holy Spirit would be given. When Jesus breathed upon them and said, *"Receive ye the Holy Ghost,"* this was three days after His death, the very day of His resurrection, and fifty days before Pentecost. On this day, the disciples received the permanent indwelling of the Holy Spirit.

They alone had the saving message the world needed. The Lord had entrusted the saving message to no one else.

Although these men were saved, experienced at the Master's hand, educated in the Master's school, and indwelt by the Holy

Spirit and although they alone had the saving message the world desperately needed, they were not yet ready to go forward to evangelize the known world. They lacked one thing. They lacked the Holy Spirit's power. Jesus said to these disciples in *Acts 1:4-5, 8: "Wait for the promise of the Father, which, saith He, ye have heard of me. For John truly baptized you with water; but ye shall be baptized with the Holy Ghost not many days hence. But ye shall receive power, after that the Holy Ghost is come upon you: and ye shall be witnesses of Me."*

In order for them to fulfill the task at hand, the disciples needed the Spirit's power. They needed more than the indwelling of the Spirit's presence; they needed an investment of the Spirit's power. They needed to be filled with the Holy Spirit. Fifty days after their indwelling and ten days after the Lord's ascension, they were filled with the Holy Spirit *(Acts 2:4)* and were now ready to reach a lost and dying world. It was only after they were filled with the Spirit that the evangelization of the world began *(Acts 2:14, 41)*. If these disciples, who were exceptionally fit for the work to which they were called, needed to be filled with the Spirit and His power, then how much more do we? There is no substitute for the power of the Holy Spirit.

The Emptiness of the Flesh

Jesus said in *John 6:63, "It is the Spirit that quickeneth; the flesh profiteth nothing."* Everything we do that is not in the energy, strength, and life-giving power of the Spirit is profitless. It is meaningless and will bring no eternal value to hearer or doer.

Not only is it profitless, but it is also deadening. To do the work of God and to preach the Word of God without the power of

God is counterproductive. *II Corinthians 3:6* says, *"The letter killeth, but the Spirit giveth life."* One of the most dangerous things that any servant of God can do is to teach or preach the Word of God without dependence upon the Spirit of God. Paul said in *I Corinthians 2:4, "And my speech and my preaching was not with enticing words of man's wisdom, but in demonstration of the Spirit and of power."* In *I Corinthians 4:20,* Paul again said, *"For the kingdom of God is not in word, but in power."* Again we are told in *I Thessalonians 1:5, "For our gospel came not unto you in word only, but also in power, and in the Holy Ghost."*

To preach or teach the Word without dependence upon the Holy Spirit is deadening. It killeth. It is counterproductive. The Spirit is the One who gives life to the Word. R. A. Torrey said, "I tremble for those who are preaching the truth, the very truth as it is in Jesus, the truth as it is recorded in the written Word of God. The truth in its simplicity, its purity, its fullness who are preaching it in 'persuasive words of man's wisdom' and not 'in demonstration of the Spirit and of power.' They are preaching it in the energy of the flesh and not in the power of the Spirit. There is nothing more death-dealing than the gospel without the Spirit's power. *"The letter killeth, but the Spirit giveth life" (II Corinthians 3:6).*[2]

C. H. Spurgeon, in his book Lectures to My Students, records the dream of the old Puritan Thomas Boston. He dreamt that while walking through town he saw the Devil preaching at the street corner. Boston thought he must be a fundamentalist for he was preaching the Gospel, telling men and women that he believed God's Word from cover to cover. The Puritan went up to him and asked, "Are you the Devil?" "Of course I am," replied the Devil. "And are you preaching the gospel?" "Yes, I am preaching the gospel," replied the Devil. "But why are you preaching the gospel?" asked the Puritan. "Because I have made this discovery: the best weapon for the damning of souls is to get men to preach the gospel without the anointing of God."

Mr. Spurgeon said that when he read this, he trembled. And so should we! To preach the Word of God without the power of the Spirit of God is to help the Devil. You may be saved and indwelt by the Spirit. You may be educated in the finest school and have years of Christian experience. You may preach the Word in boldness, zeal, and deep compassion for the souls of men, but to do it without the enabling power of the Spirit of God is profitless, deadening, and even damning. Make the power of the Holy Spirit a priority.

The Enemy of Sin

One of the primary ministries of the Holy Spirit is to give us consistent victory over the enemy of sin. *Romans 8:13* says, *"Ye through the Spirit do mortify the deeds of the body." Galatians 5:16* says, *"Walk in the Spirit, and ye shall not fulfill the lust of the flesh."* It is also the ministry of the Holy Spirit to daily conform our lives to the life of Christ. *II Corinthians 3:18* says, *"But we all with open face beholding as in a glass the glory of the Lord, are changed into the same image from glory to glory, even as by the Spirit of the Lord."* It is also the Spirit of God that brings forth Christ-like character. *Galatians 5:22-23* says, *"The fruit of the Spirit is love, joy, peace, longsuffering, gentleness, goodness, faith, meekness, temperance."* It is the Holy Spirit who *"helpeth our infirmities" (Romans 8:26).*

Do you know why we do not live each day victoriously over sin as we ought? Because we do not invite the Holy Spirit into our daily conduct, our daily conversations, or our daily conflicts. To try to live the Christian life without the Spirit's power is like a drowning man pulling at the hair of his head in an attempt to save himself. The only way to live victorious over sin is to depend upon Holy Spirit and His enabling power.

If you struggle with a lack of holiness, invite the Holy Spirit into the conflict. He is the "Spirit of holiness" *(Romans 1:4)* He will produce His holiness in you. If you struggle with a lying, gossiping tongue, invite the Holy Spirit into your conversation, for He is the "Spirit of truth" *(John 14:17)* He will produce truth in you. If you struggle with unbelief, invite the Holy Spirit into this area of your life. He is the "Spirit of faith" *(II Corinthians 4:13)* He will produce faith in you. If you lack wisdom and need to know God's mind upon a certain matter, invite the Holy Spirit in, for He is the "Spirit of wisdom" *(Ephesians 1:8)* He will give you the wisdom you need. If you lack love for others or you lack a love for the lost, invite the Holy Spirit into this area of your life, He is the "Spirit of love" *(II Timothy 1:4)* He will give you His love. If you lack discipline in reading the Word, praying, or soul winning, invite the Holy Spirit into this area of your life. He will give you the discipline you lack. Why? Because He is the "Spirit of discipline" *(II Timothy 1:7)*. It is the Holy Spirit who brings victory over the enemy of sin making His power an absolute priority.

The Evangelization of the Lost

The primary purpose of the Holy Spirit's power is for service. *Acts 1:8* says, *"But ye shall receive power, after that the Holy Ghost is come upon you: and ye shall be witnesses unto me."* The power of the Holy Spirit is not for self-enjoyment or self-glorification. It is to fulfill the Great

Commission and to advance the kingdom of God.

> *The power of the Holy Spirit is not for self-enjoyment or self-glorification. It is to fulfill the Great Commission and to advance the kingdom of God.*

Luke uses the word “witness” over twenty~nine times in the book of Acts, making it the key word and the central theme of the entire book. The word means “telling what you have seen or know.” It is telling what you know to be your own; it is telling what you know to be true. Someone said, “It is one beggar telling another beggar where to get bread.” It is one sinner telling another sinner where he can find salvation. Every Christian knows he is to be a witness, but few realize that they have available to them a special ability and power to witness. The success of the early church was not that they witnessed everywhere they went, but that every time they did witness, they did so under the Holy Spirit’s power. The key to being a successful witness is not cleverly crafted words or years of Bible training. It is a yieldedness to the Spirit and His power.

The Holy Spirit Provides the Boldness to Witness

One of the amazing features of the Spirit-filled life is the Spirit’s ability to transform the cowardly, the timid, and the fearful into the boldest witnesses for Jesus Christ. Do you remember these disciples before Pentecost? When Jesus was arrested in the Garden, they all fled. They denied any association with Christ, and even ten days before Pentecost they were hiding behind closed doors for fear of the Jews. Suddenly, they were all transformed. *Acts 4:31* says, *"And they were all filled with the Holy Ghost, and they spake the word of God with boldness."* What brought about this transformation? What brought about this change? The answer is that they were all filled with the Holy Spirit. I know of a young sixteen-year-old boy who was so timid that he would barely talk on the ordinary topics of life. But, after yielding his life to the Lord and being filled with the Spirit, he became as bold as a lion in witnessing. I watched this young man witness to people on the streets and in the parks. I watched him witness and win people next to him on a plane. I watched him witness to young and old, to rich and poor. It was the Holy Spirit's power that made the difference.

The Holy Spirit Provides the Weight to Our Witness

Jesus said in *John 15:26-27*, *"But when the Comforter is come, whom I will send unto you from the father, even the Spirit of truth, which proceedeth from the Father, he shall testify of me: And ye also shall bear witness, because ye have been with me from the beginning."* When the Spirit-filled believer witnesses, the Holy Spirit will confirm to the hearer that the words spoken are true. The Holy Spirit gives weight to my witness. In *Acts 5*, the apostles were in the temple in Jerusalem teaching the people concerning the death, burial, and resurrection of the Lord. In *Acts 5:32*, the apostles said, *"And we are his witesses of these things; and so is also the Holy Ghost, whom God hath given to them that obey Him."* In other words as they witnessed, the Holy Spirit witnessed with them and through them. What was the result of this co-witnessing? *Acts 5:33* says, *"When they heard that, they were cut to the heart, and took counsel to slay them."* The Holy Spirit gives weight to our witness; He confirms to the hearer that the words are true. He convicts and convinces the hearer of his sin, Christ's righteousness, and God's coming judgment.

Not long ago I was with a team in the Philippines doing some soul-winning training. One afternoon, my wife took a team of trainees to the park to witness. One of the ladies with my wife was very cynical. She was a faithful witness who passed out tracts, but never saw anyone saved. She came to the conclusion that one just could not win Catholics and that the people in her city were just too hard and could not be reached. In order to prove this to my wife, the trainee directed her to speak to a Catholic lady sitting on a park bench. My wife sat beside this elderly Catholic lady and engaged her in a spiritual conversation. The lady loved God and went to church every day. She was very serious in her faith, but she was lost. In less than one hour, this lady and the cynical trainee both became believers. The Catholic lady believed in Christ alone to save her from sin and hell, and the cynical trainee believed in the power of the Holy Spirit to convince and convict the hearer. The Holy Spirit gives weight to our witness.

The Holy Spirit Provides the Words to Witness

Jesus said in *John 14:26, "But the Comforter, which is the Holy Ghost, whom the Father will send in my name, He shall teach you all things, and bring all things to your remembrance, whatsoever I have said unto you."* In August 2001, I was in Johannesburg, South Africa, doing some soul-winning training. During one of the practical soul-winning times, we met a lady in the front yard of her home. I declared the gospel to her, and she saw her need to be saved. When I asked her, "Since Jesus is willing to save you, are you willing to ask Him to save you right now?" She replied, "I do not think it is appropriate to make this decision out in the open like this. This decision should be made in private or in a church–not out here." This took me by surprise, so under my breath I prayed, "Your words, Lord!" Immediately the Lord brought to my mind the story of Philip and the Ethiopian eunuch. After telling her how the Ethiopian eunuch prayed, and asked the Lord to save him while sitting out in his chariot, she said, "If it was all right with him, then it is all right with me," and she was wonderfully saved.

The Holy Spirit Provides the Enabling to Preach

In *Acts 2:4*, we are told that Peter was filled with the Holy Spirit. *Acts 2:14* records for us that great Pentecostal sermon concerning Jesus Christ's death, burial, and resurrection. The result of that sermon was that 3,000 people were saved *(Acts 2:41).* Do you realize how foolish it would have been for Peter, apart from the power of the Holy Spirit, to stand before this group of 30,000 to 40,000 religious Jews and preach to them that Jesus Christ was dead but now is alive and that He alone can save men from sin and hell? It makes absolutely no human sense to stand before people and say, "You are sinners, your sin will send you to an eternal hell, there is only one way out and that is through Jesus Christ alone!" Declaring that message makes no human sense apart from the power of the Holy Spirit energizing those words.

The Holy Spirit Provides the Ability to Lead

In *Matthew 9:37-38*, Jesus said, *"The harvest truly is plenteous, but the labourers are few; pray ye therefore the Lord of the harvest, that He will send forth labourers into His harvest."* It is the Holy Spirit who leads men and women into service. It is the Holy Spirit who leads men and women into the harvest field. It is the Holy Spirit who leads men and women to the people who need to be saved. In *Acts 8*, it was the Holy Spirit who led Philip to the Ethiopian eunuch. It was then the Holy Spirit who led him from the Gaza Desert into Azotus and Caesarea where souls were saved *(Acts 8:39-40)*. It was the Holy Spirit who sent Paul and Barnabas from the city of Antioch to the island of Cyprus and then into Asia Minor on that first missionary journey *(Acts 13:1-12)*. It was the Holy Spirit who led Paul to Troas and the Aegean Sea where he heard that Macedonian call, *"Come over . . . and help us" (Acts 16:6-10)*. It was the Holy Spirit who led Paul to Philippi, where he was led to a lady named Lydia whose heart had been opened by the Lord. Lydia and her household were saved. From Philippi, the Spirit led Paul to Thessalonica *(Acts 17:1-9)*, where in a short time, souls were saved and a vibrant church was established. From Thessalonica Paul was led by the Spirit to Berea *(Acts 17:10-15)*, and in Berea he was led to souls that were saved *(v. 12)*. From Berea, the Spirit led him to Athens *(Acts 17:16-34)*. In Athens, he was led to Dionysus and Damaris, who were saved *(v. 34)*. From Athens Paul was led by the Holy Spirit to Corinth *(18:1-8)*, and in Corinth, he was led to Crispus, who was saved *(v. 8)*. The Holy Spirit is the Lord of the harvest, and He directs and leads men and women to those who need to be saved..

An atheist who lived by C. H. Spurgeon's home was unkind to anyone who believed the Bible. On one particular morning, Spurgeon asked the Lord to guide him in what he should read for his morning devotions. He seemed strongly impressed to read the complete book of Joel. When he came to *Joel 3*, he read the third verse: *"And sold the girl for wine."* When Spurgeon checked his concordance to see how many times the word girl occurs in the Bible, he was surprised to discover that it occurred only once. When he had finished his devotions, Spurgeon decided to take a walk. After walking about a block and a half, he looked up to see the atheist's home. He went up and knocked on the door. The atheist growled and said, "What do you want?" "I would like to read the Bible to you," said Mr. Spurgeon. The atheist began his usual abuse, and then suddenly he stopped and said, "Will you tell me how often the word girl occurs in the Bible?" Mr. Spurgeon said, "Once." Then the atheist said, "Tell me where it is found and I will let you in." Spurgeon replied, *"Joel 3:3."* The atheist then said, "Tell me before I let you in, how did you know it?" Mr. Spurgeon answered, "I have only known it for two hours. In my morning devotions, I read the book of Joel." Spurgeon was let in, and within thirty minutes the atheist was on his knees asking God to save him from sin and hell.[3] The Holy Spirit provides the power to witness, to preach, and to lead believers to souls that need to be saved, making the power of the Holy Spirit an absolute priority.

At forty-five years of age, Jonathan Goforth was a successful missionary. Although successful by human standards, he longed to see "the greater works" that were promised by our Lord in *John 14:12.* He was not satisfied with simply touching the fringe when so many knew not the truth. About this time, Goforth began to receive pamphlets describing the revival in Wales. As he read the pamphlets, a new thought, a new conception, seemed

The Holy Spirit provides the power to witness, to preach, and to lead believers to souls that need to be saved, making the power of the Holy Spirit an absolute priority.

to come to him of God the Holy Spirit and His part in the conviction and conversion of men. As a result, Jonathan Goforth bought a wide-margin Chinese Bible and gave himself to a detailed study of the teaching of the Scripture on the Holy Spirit. He rose early to have uninterrupted time with his Bible. Fearing that he would break his health, one day his wife said, "Jonathan, are you not going too far on this?" Rising from his knees, he faced her with a look that she would never forget and said, "Oh, Rose, even you do not understand! I feel like one who has tapped a mine of wealth. It is so wonderful. Oh, if I could only get others to see it." What was the result of his study? He was filled with the Spirit. What was the result of this filling? One night he was speaking to a heathen audience that filled the street chapel. Goforth witnessed a stirring among the people that he had never seen before as he spoke on the verse *"who his own self bare our sins in his own body on the tree."* Conviction of sin was written on every face. When he asked for decisions, practically all responded. Then turning about, seeking for one of the evangelists to carry on, he found the whole band of them standing in a row with awed looks on their faces. Then one whispered, "Brother, He for whom we have prayed for so long, was here in very deed tonight." During the days that followed, at every center where Goforth preached the gospel, men and women came seeking salvation.[4] Are you filled with the Spirit? Do you know His power?

Be Filled with the Spirit

Ephesians 5:18

CHAPTER EIGHT

Be Filled with the Spirit

Ephesians 5:18

If you were to ask me to define what a Christian is in three words or less, I would say as Paul did in ***Colossians 1:27, "Christ in you."*** That is a very simple, very biblical, very accurate, and very profound definition of a Christian: "Christ in you." John Wesley said a Christian is "the life of God in the soul of man."

Sadly, many people misunderstand what a Christian truly is. Some think being a Christian is simply following Jesus. However, many who follow Jesus claiming to be His disciples are not. Some think being a Christian is abiding by the teachings of Christ. But there are many moral people and good people who conform their lives to the teachings of Christ who are not Christians. Some think that a Christian is one who goes to church on Sunday, has been baptized, reads the Bible, and gives financially to the church. However, none of these things makes one a Christian; neither do they define what a Christian is. A Christian is one who has the life of God in his soul; he is one who has Christ dwelling in him. A Christian is one who is rightly related to Christ.

The key and the secret to living that abundant Christian life, that fruitful and victorious life, is letting the Spirit who indwells you control you.

Once a person becomes a Christian, the next step–and it is the most important step–is to be rightly related to the Holy Spirit. The moment one puts his faith and trust in Jesus Christ, the Holy Spirit immediately indwells him. When you asked Jesus to save you from the penalty of sin, at that same time you received the Spirit of God. You were permanently indwelt by the Spirit and received at that moment all the Holy Spirit you will ever receive. We do not receive some of the Holy Spirit at salvation and some later. We do not receive the Holy Spirit in parts. At salvation we are permanently and completely indwelt.

The key and the secret to living that abundant Christian life, that fruitful and victorious life, is letting the Spirit who indwells you control you. The secret of the spiritual life is not your getting more of the Spirit but rather your allowing the indwelling Spirit to get more of you.

Many years ago a group of pastors were discussing whether or not to invite the evangelist D. L. Moody to their city. The success and fame of the evangelist were brought to the attention of the men. One unimpressed minister commented, "Does Mr. Moody have a monopoly on the Holy Spirit?" Another man replied, "No, but it seems that the Holy Spirit has a monopoly on Mr. Moody." That is the key to living the abundant, victorious Christian life. It is allowing the indwelling

Holy Spirit to monopolize you. If you are going to be monopolized and controlled by the Spirit, then you must "be filled with the Spirit."

The Characteristics of Being Filled with the Spirit

Divine Command

The words *be filled* in *Ephesians 5:18* are in the imperative mood in the Greek, which means "to be filled with the Spirit." It is a command, not an option for the Christian. It is not something one can take or leave. It is a mandate from almighty God to every child of God.

The most urgent and most important command in the Bible is *Acts 17:30*. God *"now commandeth all men everywhere to repent."* But the most important and urgent command for every child of God is *Ephesians 5:18: "Be filled with the Spirit."* To disobey this command is as much an act of disobedience as it is to be drunk with wine. Both are commands. To disobey the command to be filled with the Spirit is the same as disobeying the command to sobriety. A drunk Christian is an awful sight. He is a disgrace to the cause and makes a mockery of the cross. However, in the eyes of God, there is no distinction between the drunk Christian and the unfilled Christian.

This command to be filled with the Spirit is demonstration of God's love for us. When we are living under the Spirit's control, we are living under the Spirit's protection. We will know His power, His leading, and all His blessings. It is God's love that makes this a command. God knows that to live outside of the Holy Spirit's control is to live a defeated, weak, and frustrated Christian life.

Decisively Corporate

The command *be filled* is plural in the Greek language, which means the filling of the Spirit is for everyone. It is not something that is reserved for the pastor, the preacher, or the deacons of the church. The filling of the Spirit is for everyone. It does not matter how old or how young. It is not only for the rich and famous or the highly educated. It is for the corporate body, for every believer. It is God's desire that every believer in every church be filled with the Spirit.

Demands Consent

The command *be filled* is also passive, which means being filled with the Spirit is not something you do but rather something you allow the Holy Spirit to do to you. You are the object of the action. You are the one being filled; you are not filling yourself with the Spirit. You are to allow the Spirit to fill you. The filling of the Spirit is entirely the work of the Spirit Himself, but He works only through our willing consent. He only fills a vessel that desires to be filled.

Definitely Continual

The phrase *be filled* is in the present tense, which means being filled with the Spirit is a day-by-day, moment-by-moment, submission to the Spirit's control. It is not a once-and-for-all experience. It is a day-by-day, moment-by-moment, constant yieldedness to the indwelling Holy Spirit. Every Christian at any given moment is either filled with the Spirit or filled by the flesh; it all depends upon your yieldedness. There is no middle ground. You are either carnally controlled or Spirit controlled.

In *Matthew 16:13-23*, Peter was one moment under the control of the Spirit and the next under the control of the flesh. In *verses 15-17*, Jesus asked Peter, *"But whom say ye that I am?"* Peter answered saying, *"Thou are the Christ, the Son of the living God."* Then Jesus commended him saying, *"For flesh and blood hath not revealed it unto thee, but My Father which is in heaven."* Here Peter gives evidence of being filled with the Spirit for that which he knew was taught to him by the Spirit. Then a few moments later *(vv. 21-23)*, Jesus reveals to His disciples that He must suffer many things and die. Peter immediately rebukes the Lord, and the Lord rebukes Satan, who put the thought into Peter's mind. Peter gave evidence of being under the control of the flesh.

The filling of the Spirit is not a once-and-for-all event, but a daily, moment-by-moment yieldedness and walk with the Spirit. This is clearly seen in the example of the early church. In *Acts 2:4*, the church was filled with the Holy Spirit at Pentecost; then in *Acts 4:31*, they all (referring to the same people) were filled again. *In Acts 2:4*, Peter was one of those at Pentecost and one of those who were filled with the Spirit. Yet he was filled again in *Acts 4:8* and also again in *4:31*. In *Acts 9:17*, Paul yielded himself to the Holy Spirit and was filled. Then he was filled again in *Acts 13:9*, and again in *Acts 13:52*, Peter, Paul, and all the disciples were filled with the Spirit. The Holy Spirit's filling is a moment-by-moment filling as we daily yield ourselves to Him. God commands that we be continually under the Spirit's control.

Defined Control

The word "filled" means to "be controlled by; to be dominated by." The Christian is to be controlled by the Spirit, as dominated by the Spirit as a drunken man is by his alcohol. The word *excess* carries the idea of "abandonment." When a person is drunk with alcohol, he abandons self, common sense, and reason. He leaves his fears and inhibitions and often becomes as bold as a lion. He is like that quiet little guy who rarely speaks and almost goes unnoticed. However get some alcohol into his system and what a difference! He loses his fears, abandons common sense, talks with everyone and anyone, sings, laughs, and jokes. Often he becomes as bold as a lion, sometimes foolishly picking a fight with the biggest guy around.

I heard a story about two drunken men. One of them decided that he was going to jump out of the window and fly around the block. When his friend later came to see him in the hospital, the much-bandaged and broken patient said to this friend, "Why did you not stop me? Why did you let me do it?" His friend replied, "Because I thought you could."

Why does a drunken man behave as he does? He does it because he is under the influence of alcohol. Likewise, a Christian is to be as filled with - as controlled by - the Holy Spirit as the drunken man is by his alcohol. In *Luke 4:28*, the Bible says that the people of Nazareth were *"filled with wrath"* at Jesus when He challenged them for their unbelief. They did not just get filled with rage and walk away. Their rage totally controlled them, for they tried to push Jesus off the cliff. In *Acts 13:45,* the Jews in Antioch became *"filled with envy"* at the success of Paul and Barnabas. They were so controlled by jealousy that they began to attack the two men.

That is what it means to be "filled with the Spirit". It means that you are so controlled, so dominated by the Spirit that another controls your will and your desires. Just as alcohol controls the drunk, just as rage controls the angered, the Spirit is to control the Christian.

Keep in mind that the Holy Spirit is not a force. He is not a feeling; He is a Person. To be filled with the Spirit is to be filled with the Person of the Holy Spirit. It is the Person of the Holy Spirit controlling my person. When I surrender the control of my life to Him, allowing the Spirit to control me, He in turn imparts to my life His power and His personality which is a power and a personality that can only be known as I yield myself to His control. God commands that all Christians consent to His continual control in their lives.

God commands that all Christians consent to His continual control in their lives.

The Condition of Being Filled with the Spirit

There are three divinely inspired conditions for the filling of the Spirit. When these three conditions are met, we will be under the Spirit's control, and we will know the Spirit's ministry working in us and through us.

Confession of Sin

Ephesians 4:30 says, *"And grieve not the Holy Spirit of God."* The word grieve means "to cause pain; to sorrow; to hurt deeply." Because the Holy Spirit is a Person, we can cause Him pain and hurt Him deeply. Whenever we do anything that is contrary to His character, we grieve Him. For example, the Bible says the Holy Spirit is the *"Spirit of truth" (John 14:17),* so anything that is false, deceitful, or hypocritical grieves Him. If there is a lie in your life, then do not expect to be Spirit filled until that lie is confessed. He is the *"Spirit of faith" (II Corinthians 4:13)*, so any doubt, unbelief, distrust, worry, or anxiety grieves Him. If you doubt His Word, if you worry over your children or remove over your business, you are grieving the Holy Spirit and He cannot fill you. He is the *"Spirit of grace" (Hebrews 10:29)*. Anything that is hard, bitter, unforgiving, without grace or without gratitude grieves Him. If you are holding something against someone, if there is bitterness in your life, if you spend your days murmuring and complaining about this and that, do not pray to be filled with the Spirit until you confess this as sin. He is the *"Spirit of holiness" (Romans 1:4)*. Anything that is unclean, defiling, or degrading grieves Him. If you are watching, reading, or listening to things that you know God hates, such as movies or television shows, books or magazines that are filled with illicit sex or profanity, you are grieving the Spirit. You cannot do what you know God hates and be filled with the Spirit at the same time. To think you can indicates your own deception. He is the *"Spirit of wisdom" (Ephesians 1:17)*. Ignorance, conceit, and arrogance grieve Him. To be ignorant of the Bible while being proud of your knowledge is to grieve Him. He is the *"Spirit of power, love, and discipline" (II Timothy 1:7)*, our weakness, our fruitlessness, and our lack of self-control grieve Him. He is the *"Spirit of life" (Romans 8:2)*, anything with the savor of indifference, luke-warmness, dullness, or deadness grieves Him. He is grieved at our half-hearted attempts to serve Him. He is the *"Spirit of glory" (I Peter 4:14)*, anything that is worldly, earthly, or fleshly grieves Him.

All sin grieves the Spirit and hinders the Spirit's filling. Whenever we sin, whether it be a burst of anger, a lustful glance, an act of adultery, or any willful act of sin we grieve the Spirit and place ourselves under the control of the flesh. Sin destroys spirituality. It hinders the Spirit-filled life and it grieves and pains the Spirit deeply. Whenever a Christian tolerates known sin in his life, the Spirit who dwells within him is grieved. The Spirit's filling is not dependent upon living a sinless life. It is dependent upon willingness to confess all known sin.

Confession is the key. Confession of all known sin places us under the Spirit's control. All of us must keep short accounts with God and men. We must consistently be willing to confess all known sin. This will ensure the Spirit's constant control.

A young man came to a preacher and said, "I have lost the Holy Spirit." The preacher replied, "You have not lost the Holy Spirit, but you may have grieved Him with some particular sin." The young man could not think of any particular sin in his life that stood between himself and God. The preacher asked, "What about your relationship with your parents?" In response the young man said, "Well, it is not the best." The preacher dug deeper and asked, "Do you honor your father?" The young man agreed that he had sinned in this area. Then the preacher said, "Why don't you go home and make things right, and if you have sinned, confess it." The young man did that, and a few days later he came back with a broad smile and said, "Fellowship restored." He was not just referring to fellowship with his parents, but his fellowship with the Holy Spirit was also restored.

When the Christian tolerates known sin in his life, the Holy Spirit has to abandon His ministry of working *through* us and has must turn to a pleading ministry to us. When we tolerate known sin in our lives, no longer is the Spirit producing Christ-like character, empowering our service, or enabling us to live victoriously over sin. He must now turn His attention to *us* and convict *us* of sin, righteousness, and

God's coming judgment *(John 16:7-11)*. The first condition to living the Spirit-filled life is to confess all known sin.

Compliance to the Spirit

I Thessalonians 5:19 says, *"Quench not the Spirit."* The word *quench* means "to suppress; to stifle." We quench and stifle the Spirit and His working when we fail to yield ourselves to Him. When we say "No!" to God, when we are unwilling to do His will, when we resist His working and refuse to yield ourselves to His control, then we quench the Spirit.

One thing that keeps Christians from living that Spirit-filled life is the failure to "yield ourselves to God." The Scripture is constantly exhorting us to do so. *Romans 6:13* says, *"Neither yield your members as instruments of unrighteousness unto sin: but yield yourselves unto God, as those that are alive from the dead."* The word translated as "yield" is in the aorist tense and means we are to yield ourselves once and for all to God. There should be a point in your walk with God when you make a definite yielding of your entire life, body, soul, mind, and will to God. *Romans 12:1* says, *"Present* [yield] *our bodies a living sacrifice, holy, acceptable unto God."* The word "present" refers to a definite point in our lives when we yielded ourselves to God. You will never know the Spirit's filling until you willingly surrender your will to the will of God.

The greatest enemy of the Spirit-filled life is the self-directed life. Jesus said in *Matthew 6:24, "No man can serve two masters."* If self is on the throne of your life, then self is the master and the Spirit is quenched. The key to the Spirit-filled life is to exchange masters; yield yourself and the self-run life to the Spirit and allow Him to run your life. It is a complete, absolute surrender. It is surrendering your will for His will. It is taking the will of God as the rule for your life. One reason so few live the Spirit-filled life is that they are serving two masters.

Sam Jones, that great American evangelist, was once holding an evangelistic campaign in the state of Texas. As a love offering for his services, the Texans gave him a train carload of unbroken broncos (wild horses). Sam lived in the city of Philadelphia. He sold all the horses but one, which he was going to keep for his son. He called a cowboy and asked him how much it would cost to break his wild horse so that his son could ride it. The cowboy said, "Fifteen dollars." The deal was made. The cowboy said he would have the horse back in two weeks. After two weeks passed, the horse was back. Mr. Jones decided that he should first try the horse, so he began to mount. The cowboy came running up, saying, "Stop! Stop! The horse has only been broken on one side and you are mounting on the wrong side." "Well, that will never do," said Mr. Jones. "How much will you charge me to break him on the other side." "Another fifteen dollars," said the cowboy, and off the horse went. Two weeks later the horse returned, and Mr. Jones asked, "Is the horse broken?" "Yes," replied the cowboy. "Both sides?" asked Mr. Jones. "Yes, sir! Both sides."[1]

Is this not the reason so few are Spirit-filled? They are broken on only one side. They have surrendered one side of their lives, but not both. They will do this, but not that. They will go here, but not there. They are willing to do anything as long as it fits their schedules or their criteria. To be Spirit-filled demands an absolute surrender of your will for His. Once that initial act of surrender is made, there must be that daily surrender of your will to His will.

John Sung was without a doubt one of the greatest evangelists of all times. He, like everyone whom God uses, had to make that great exchange and yield his will and life to the will and control of the Father. When John sung was twenty-seven years old, he had just finished a Ph.D. in chemistry from Ohio State University. His future was promising, and his prospects were bright. As he was traveling back to China, God got hold of his heart and Dr. Sung knew he had a choice to make and it would certainly be his will or God's will. The choice was not easy. He had just spent six years in the United States studying, and his abilities were greatly needed back in China. But John Sung surrendered, and he surrendered absolutely. He went on deck of the ship that was carrying him home to China. There he cast his diplomas into the sea. This act of surrender was the turning point in his life and ministry. Within the next few years, God used John Sung to bring revival fire to China, Taiwan, Malaysia, Singapore, Indonesia, and the Philippines. In a span of three years, he won over 100,000 people to the Lord. Missionary William E. Schubert said this: "I have heard almost all the great preachers from 1910 to 1976, including R. A. Torrey, Billy Sunday, Henry Jowett, and others. Yet John Sung surpassed them all in pulpit power, attested by amazing and enduring results."[2] To be filled with the Spirit, there must be confession of all known sin and an absolute surrender of your will for His.

Confidence in the Spirit

Galatians 5:16 says, *"Walk in the Spirit, and ye shall not fulfil the lust of the flesh."* To walk means "to rely upon; to depend on." To *walk in the Spirit* means "to have an attitude of dependence on the Spirit's power and ability." It means to depend upon the One who dwells within you. There are many verses in the Bible that remind us of the need to depend upon the Spirit. *Romans 8:14* says, *"For as many as are led by the Spirit of God, they are the sons of God." Galatians*

5:18 says that we are to be "led of the Spirit." *Galatians 5:25* says that we are to *"live in the Spirit."* Each of these words, *walk, live, led* means to be totally dependent upon Him. To be filled with the Spirit is to be depending upon the Holy Spirit's power His enabling, and His ability in every area of your life. The Spirit-filled life is the exchanged life; it is exchanging my will for His will and living absolutely dependent upon Him. Paul said it this way: *"...nevertheless I live; yet not I, but Christ liveth in me* [surrender], *and the life which I now live in the flesh, I live by the faith* [dependence] *of the Son of God,"* (Galatians 2:20).

To be filled with the Spirit is to be depending upon the Holy Spirit's power, His enabling, and His ability in every area of your life.

The Consequences of Being Filled with the Spirit

The Spirit-filled Christian is the supernatural Christian. There are things about his life that you cannot explain apart from the divine working of God. He is not one who simply lives a good life, although he will. He is not one who lives better than the rest, although he may. He is one who has the mark of the supernatural about his life and work. His life cannot be explained apart from God. He lives beyond human ability. There are several consequences of a Spirit-filled Christian.

Christ-like Character

One of the primary characteristics of a Spirit-filled believer is that his life will begin to manifest the character of Christ.

John 16:14 says, *"He* [the Holy Spirit] *shall glorify Me* [Jesus]." The word "glorify" means "to show; manifest; display; make known." The evidence that the Holy Spirit is in control of the believer's life is the life will begin to manifest the character of Christ. The Holy Spirit takes the yielded believer and begins to conform his life into the image of Christ *(Romans 8:29; II Corinthians 3:18).* This conforming and transforming work of the Spirit is so great that the yielded believer begins to live Christ's life. He beings to walk as Jesus walked and love as Jesus loved. He has Christ's joy, His peace, His patience, His gentleness, His goodness, His faithfulness, His meekness, and His self-control. He begins to have the Lord's desires and to share the Lord's burdens. Someone may be thinking, "Impossible! There is no way I could live like that." That is precisely the point. It is not something you do but some-thing you allow the Spirit to do through you. The Holy Spirit indwells you to conform you into His image. *II Corinthians 3:18* says, *"But we all, with open face beholding as in a glass the glory of the Lord, are changed into the same image from glory to glory, even as by the Spirit of the Lord."* The Spirit of God takes the Word of God and conforms those who are yielded to Him into His very same image. As I yield myself to the Spirit, His life becomes my life, His personality my personality. "I am in Him and He is in me."

When you place a piece of iron in the fire, soon that fire begins to penetrate the iron and you have not only the iron in the fire but the fire in the iron. The two have so co-mingled and interpenetrated one another so as to have become one. The same is true with the believer and the Holy Spirit. When a Christian is filled with the Spirit, the Holy Spirit penetrates and fills his personality so that he becomes experientially one with Him. This oneness brings about a Christ-like character.

Consistent Victory over Sin

The only way we will ever be consistently victorious over sin is to be filled with the Spirit. *Galatians 5:16* says, "*Walk in the Spirit, and ye shall not fulfil the lust of the flesh.*" *Romans 8:13* says, "*If ye through the Spirit do mortify the deeds of the body, ye shall live.*" *Romans 8:2* says, "*The law of the Spirit of life in Christ Jesus hath made me free from the law of sin and death.*" We have been freed not only from the penalty of sin but also from the power of sin. However, having been freed, it is still sin's desire to pull us down. The only answer to the downward pull of sin is the counter-acting influence of the Holy Spirit. Far greater and more powerful than the law of sin is the law of the indwelling Spirit. Far greater and more powerful than the flesh is the power of the Holy Spirit. To have constant victory over sin is to be constantly filled with the Spirit.

Courageous Power in Service

Only the Spirit-filled believer will faithfully, effectively, and powerfully serve God. In *Acts 1:8* we read, "*Ye shall receive power, after that the Holy Ghost is come upon you: and ye shall be witnesses unto me.*" This is the testimony of the book of Acts. It was the filling of the Spirit that empowered the early church in witness and service for the Lord.

Being filled with the Spirit changes the most cowardly into the bold. Remember Peter, that cowardly believer who denied the Lord three times and ran away, fearful of being associated with Christ *(Matthew 26:69-75)*? In *Acts 2:4*, Peter was filled with the Spirit, and in *Acts 2:14* we see him standing before thousands proclaiming the gospel of Christ. What made the difference? He was filled with the Spirit.

Being filled with the Spirit gives courage to spread the Word and witness for Christ. In *Acts 4:31*, the church was filled with the Spirit. The result was they witnessed boldly. In *Acts 6:3,7*, the deacons were filled with the Spirit. As a result, they spread the Word. In *Acts 9:7, 20,* Paul was filled with the Spirit. As a result, he spread the Word and witnessed. A Spirit-filled believer is a witnessing believer.

Being filled with the Spirit makes service for God successful. Peter's success on the Day of Pentecost, when 3,000 people were saved, was the result of the Spirit's enabling. We read in *Acts 6:1-7* that the church needed leaders, so they chose seven men. The main requirement of leadership was that they had to be *"full of the Holy Spirit."* Because the church had Spirit-filled leadership, *"the word of God increased; and the number of the disciples multiplied in Jerusalem greatly."* Being filled with the Spirit gives courage, power and success in service.

In the late 1800s, D. L. Moody and Ira Sankey were holding evangelistic meetings in England. They decided to reserve one night of meetings for atheists, skeptics, and freethinkers. At the time, Charles Bradlaugh was the champion of the atheistic league. Bradlaugh took Moody's challenge and closed all his clubs so that some 5,000 atheists could attend the meeting. The service began as usual. After a few songs, Mr. Moody asked for a favorite from the crowd which brought only laughter, for atheists do not know any hymns. Mr. Moody preached on the subject, "Their rock is not our rock." At the close of the meeting, Mr. Moody said, "Let's stand and sing 'Only trust Him, only trust Him,' and while we do, the ushers will open the doors, and any man that wants to leave can do so." But no one left. They all stood and sang the hymn. No one responded to the invitation. Mr. Moody asked them all to be seated again, and he began to explain the words receive, believe, trust, and take. After explaining what it means to receive Jesus, he said, "Who will receive Him? Stand and say 'I will.' " One man stood and said, "I can't." Then Mr. Moody went on to explain what it means "to believe in Jesus." When he finished, he said, "Who will believe in Jesus? Stand and say 'I will.' " Then the leader of the atheistic league stood and said, "I won't." Overcome with tears, Mr. Moody said, "It is 'I will' or 'I won't' for every man here tonight." Then he turned to the story of the prodigal son and began to preach [his fourth sermon]. When he finished, he said, "Men, there in the middle of the auditorium you have your champion who said 'I won't' to Jesus. I want everyone who believes he is right to stand up and say, 'I won't.' " There was perfect silence; no man rose. Then Mr. Moody said, "Now, who will say 'I will' to Jesus?" Immediately the power of God's Spirit fell, and five hundred men stood to their feet and said, "I will. I will." In the next two nights, over two thousand atheists were converted to Christ.[3] What God the Spirit did through D. L. Moody is what God the Spirit wants to do though you today.

Will you say "I will" to the Holy Spirit? Will you confess all known sin? Will you surrender your will to His will? Will you depend upon the Holy Spirit? Will you be filled?

The Great Commission

Matthew 28:16-20

CHAPTER NINE

The Great Commission

Matthew 28:16-20

Planet earth now strains under the weight of over six billion people. Every time the earth finishes her orbit around the sun, 200,000 more people are added to this planet. Demographers tell us that within our lifetime earth will reach her ultimate population size of thirty billion people.

It is hard for us to visualize the word billion. Newspapers report people making, spending, and losing billions of dollars every day. When we hear of Bill Gates making 2.8 billion dollars a day or Ted Turner giving away 1 billion dollars to the United Nations, we have a hard time comprehending such a figure. It lost its impact. But, if we remove the figure from the realm of money and place it in the realm of time, it takes on a more realistic perspective. For example, one billion days ago, earth had not yet been created. One billion hours ago, Genesis had not yet been written. One billion minutes ago, Christ was still walking on this planet. One billion seconds ago, the atomic bomb had not been dropped.

As difficult as it is for us to visualize a billion, the fact remains that there are today six billion people on the earth. Sadly, out of these 6 billion people, 4.5 billion are still unsaved. They are without Christ. Even sadder is the fact that of these 4.5 billion, 2.5 billion have never heard, even once, the message of the cross.

Every minute, 70 people die and are ushered into eternity. That is 4,200 people every hour, 180,000 every day, and approximately 40 million a year. Out of these 40 million souls, 800,000 are saved and 39.2 million die without hope. They go to a Christless eternity.

Jesus had these unsaved multitudes in mind when He spoke the words in *Matthew 28:18-20: "All power is given unto Me in heaven and in earth. Go ye therefore, and teach all nations, baptizing them in the name of the Father, and of the Son, and of the Holy Ghost: Teaching them to observe all things whatsoever I have commanded you: and, lo, I am with you alway, even unto the end of the world."* In speaking these words, He was giving to His disciples and His church its mission. He was revealing to the church and its people the very reason for their existence. If we understand the book of Matthew but fail to understand this closing passage, we have missed the point of the entire book. This passage, known as the Great Commission, is the climax and the major focal point of the entire New Testament. Even in a broader sense, it is the climax and focal point of the Bible.

It has never been God's desire for any man to perish. He desires that every man be saved. When Adam and Eve sinned in the Garden, God, seeing their sin, came and sought them. It was God who sought Adam and Eve, not Adam and Eve who sought God. God came into the Garden crying out, "Adam, where are you?" God saved them and restored them. When man began to separate himself further from God, God raised up a nation called Israel to be a witness to a lost world. When Israel failed to accept her long-awaited Messiah, God called out a church as His chosen instrument to reach a lost and dying world. Reaching a lost world has always been the primary function and mission of the church.

Doubtlessly the central message of Scripture is *"Jesus came to seek and to save the lost."* That is the mission of the church. Do you remember Jesus' words in *John 20:21, "As My Father hath sent Me, even so send I you"*? In other words, "As the Father sent Me into the world to win the world, so I send you into the world to win the world." This message is our mission.

If we were to take a survey in the average church and ask, "What is the mission of the church?", we would likely get a variety of answers. Some would say "fellowship" is the primary function of the church; others would say "Bible study" is the primary mission of the church. Some would claim that "praise and worship" are the supreme functions of the church. But, if these things were the primary function of the church, Christ would have taken us to heaven the moment we were saved because we can do each of these things better in heaven than we could ever do on earth. In heaven we would have no distractions. We would be unhindered by sin. We would have full knowledge. There is only one reason the Lord allows us to remain on earth: to continue His work of seeking to save the lost. The only thing we can do on earth that we will never be able to do in heaven is to win souls.

The central message of Scripture is "Jesus came to seek and to save the lost." The mission of the church is the same.

If the church is not seeking to win the lost, what divine reason does it have to exist? If each of us individually is not seeking to win the lost, what divine reason do we have to exist? We might as well go to heaven and be free from this sin-cursed, sin-tainted world.

Fellowship, Bible study, and worship are important functions of the church, but only because they are the instruments that God uses to prepare us and help us to fulfill this mission of winning the lost to Christ.

The Mandate of the Mission *(vv. 19-20a)*

Soul winning is not a spiritual gift. It is not optional nor is it something we can give or take. It is a mandate from God to every believer. It is something that God demands we do. You can get on the bus and see the signs that say, "No eating, no smoking, no drinking," and you may say to yourself, "Says who? On whose authority?" The preacher may preach, and a Christian may ask, "Says who? On whose authority?" But when it comes to soul winning, the answer is clear: on God's authority. We must work at making disciples simply because God demands it. It is a matter of obedience.

It Is an Active Mandate

"Go therefore and make disciples." "Make disciples" is the command. The little word "go" tells us how to do it. To win souls, we must simply "go after them." It is not enough to simply pray for souls to be saved. While we should pray, prayer alone is not enough. It is neither enough to simply live a good and godly life before others hoping that a good testimony will point men and women to Christ. To win souls, we must go after them.

Several years ago, a man was saved during an evangelistic campaign in the Pacific Northwest. When he told his boss about it, his employer was thrilled and said, "That's great! I'm a Christian, and I have been praying for you for years." The new believer was shocked and said, "Why did you not tell me you were a Christian? You were the very reason I have not been interested in the gospel all these years." "How can that be?" the boss wondered. "I have done my very best to live the Christian life around you." "That is the whole point," the man replied. "You had lived such a model life without telling me that it was Christ who made the difference that I convinced myself that if you could live such a good life without Christ, I could too."[1]

It was Jesus who said, *"Go out into the highways and hedges, and compel them to come in" (Luke 14:21-23).* It was Paul who said, *"How then shall they call on Him in whom they have not believed? And how shall they believe in Him of whom they have not heard? And how shall they hear without a preacher? And how shall they preach, except they be sent? As it is written, How beautiful are the feet of them that preach the gospel of peace, and bring glad tidings of good things!" (Romans 10:14-15).* It was Jesus who went after Andrew and won him. It was Andrew who went after Philip and won him. It was Philip who went after the Ethiopian eunuch and won him. If we are going to fulfill this mission, we must go after souls.

Several years ago a Christian lady brought her unsaved Buddhist mother to our church family camp. This mother had never been exposed to Christianity and had never before been in a Christian environment. At the invitation and pleading of her daughter, the mother joined this all-Christian camp. The speaker preached ten messages all on the Christian life. Not one of the messages was directed toward the unsaved. This lady sat through every message and heard all the truth. On the last night, the speaker spoke on the subject *"The fields are white unto harvest,"* challenging Christians to go after souls. He gave an invitation for the unsaved to be saved, but no one responded. After the service, everyone retired to their rooms for the evening. One of the Christian ladies at the camp became burdened for this unsaved lady. Being led by the Holy Spirit, she went to her room. She knocked and when the unsaved lady opened the door, she said, "Come reap me. I'm white already unto harvest!" That Christian lady had the joy of leading that unsaved lady to the Lord. There are people all around us just like her, who will not be reached until we, in obedience to this mandate, go after souls.

It Is an All-Encompassing Mandate

We are to make disciples of *all nations*. Your responsibility does not end at your doorstep. It includes all men in all nations. Do you realize today that there are some 11,000 people-groups around the world that have never heard the gospel even once? There are 8,500 languages into which the Word of God has not yet been translated. I live in what is called the 10/40 window. This 10/40 window is the least evangelized area of the world. Ninety-seven percent of the people in this area are unsaved. It is the most populated and most needy, but also the least reached, area on earth. There is one Christian for every 2,250 people in this window.[2] In Bali, Indonesia, there are 3.8 million people with less than one percent being Christians. The whole Bible was translated in Balinese for the first time in 1990. The world's largest unreached people-group is the Sundanese from West Java, Indonesia. They number 31 million people with nearly all being Islamic. In the sixteenth century, the Muslim leader Hamid said, "I believe we can win the Sundanese." He sent Muslim missionaries and successfully converted the people.[3]

If the world in which we live is going to be reached, we who have the truth must take it to those who do not. It must be taken across the street and across the seas. When we, in obedience do it, we will find people ready and waiting to be saved. All it takes is one person burdened to take the gospel. All it takes is one person burdened to reach one person.

Robert Morrison became burdened for the Chinese, and in 1807, he became the first Protestant missionary to China since the Nestorians 900 years earlier. When Mr. Morrison stepped foot on the shores of China, there were very few, if any, Christians in that land. Less than 200 years later, reports say that between 60 and 80 million Christians now live in China, and twenty-five percent of them were saved in the last few years.

It was Adoniram Judson, who in 1813 became burdened for the mysterious and unreached land of Burma. He won to Christ a Karen man who worked for him in his home in Burma. The Karen man, now a Christian, became burdened for his own people. Mr. Judson sent him with George and Sarah Broadman back to his people. From the moment they stepped foot into the village, they won souls. Thousands and thousands were saved. The Karen people soon became burdened for the Kachin people and took to them the gospel. In a span of ninety years, 250,000 Kachin were saved. Why? Because one man got burdened. He understood the all-encompassing demand of this mandate.

It was William Carey who became burdened for India and sowed the first gospel seeds there. By the time of Mr. Carey's death, over 200,000 copies of the Bible had been sent out in over twenty different languages.

We, who know the truth, must take this truth to others if this mission of the church is going to be fulfilled.

On the Black River in Vietnam lives a group of people called the Black Tai. Several years ago, one Black Tai received Christ while in prison. Once released, he began sharing the Good News with his neighbors. Before long, more than 750 Black Tai people came to Christ. Since then, the church has been growing quickly. Entire villages have been converted. Thousands have come to know Christ and Bibles in the Black Tai language have been distrubuted.[4] Why? Because one man got burdened for others. He understood the demand of God's mandate. It is an active mandate, an all-encompassing mandate. We, who know the truth, must take this truth to others if this mission of the church is going to be fulfilled.

It Is an Absolute Mandate

"Baptizing them . . . teaching them." Soul winning is not complete until the convert is inspired to obedience. Discipleship is not just a fire escape from hell and a ladder to heaven. It involves inspiring that one to obedience. The first step of obedience a new convert can take is the step of baptism, which is the public testimony of one's faith in Christ. It is a picture of his salvation. Baptism pictures his death, burial to sin, and resurrection to new life in Christ. This baptism is not an option for the new convert; it is something the Lord commands and requires all to do. To deny the right of baptism is to disobey the Lord. Secondly, we are to teach the new convert. One reason so many new converts fall away is because

we never get them involved in the teaching ministry of the church. We do not provide proper follow-up and proper discipleship.

Not long ago, my wife and I were invited to a church anniversary. The couple we rode in the car with had invited a friend of theirs, a young lady who was unsaved. During lunch, my wife became burdened for the young lady's soul and went to talk with her. She was open to the message of the cross and trusted Christ as her Savior. The couple who brought her was very excited about their friend's salvation. They turned to my wife and asked, "Now that our friend is saved, what should we do?" The answer was to get her involved in discipleship, inspire obedience, and get her into church.

The Means to the Mission *(v. 18)*

Jesus said, *"All power is given unto me in heaven and in earth."* If this mission is going to be accomplished, we must depend upon the Lord's authority. His power and His authority have been delegated to us in three ways.

He Gave Us the Spirit of God

Acts 1:8 says, *"But ye shall receive power, after that the Holy Ghost is come upon you: and ye shall be witnesses unto me."* Why did the Lord give us His power? He gave it to enable and empower our witness. Do you know why we need His power? Because the Spirit does what we cannot do! In *John 16:7-11*, we are told that the Spirit convicts men of sin, righteousness, and God's coming judgment. This is something we cannot do, It is something the Spirit does through us.

Several years ago, we were out soul winning. One of our young ladies knocked on the door of a man and handed him a flyer inviting him to an upcoming evangelistic meeting. As she turned to walk away, she felt prompted by the Holy Spirit to talk to this man about his salvation. Doing so, within a few minutes, the man began to weep. He was broken over his sin. Now what was that? It was not her charisma, nor was it her golden tongue or her dynamic personality. It was the Holy Spirit empowering her witness. The Holy Spirit can take anyone and make that one an effective and powerful witness.

He Gave Us the Word of God

Referring to the Word of God, Paul says that the gospel is *"the power of God unto salvation to every one that believeth" (Romans 1:16).* When we say you cannot merely witness to the lost and expect them to be saved but must first disprove evolution; when we say it is not enough to declare the Gospel but must first discredit false religions as well as prove the existence of God and truth of the Bible...that is unbelief and distrust in the power of the Gospel.

When Jonathan Goforth went to China, an old, experienced missionary came to him with this advice: "Do not attempt to speak of Jesus the first time when you are preaching to the unsaved. The Chinese have a prejudice against the name of Jesus. You must first confine all your efforts to demolishing their false gods. If you are given a second opportunity, you may then bring in the name of Jesus." To which Mr. Goforth replied rather excitedly, "Never, never, never. The gospel that saved the down-and-out in the slums of Toronto is the same gospel that can save these Chinese sinners." From the very first, although speaking in broken Chinese, Jonathan Goforth preached Christ crucified, buried, and resurrected. And from the very first he saw souls saved.[5] Later in life, a young missionary up-start asked Mr. Goforth the secret of his soulwinning power. Mr. Goforth said, "I just give God a chance to speak to souls through His own Word."[6]

Not long ago, I was helping with a new church in Singapore. A young professional man, a brother of one of the members, came to church. I had not met the man before. When he entered the church, he came straight up to me, introduced himself, and said, "I'm an atheist, and I do not believe any of this Christianity business. You will never convince me that it is true." He came for about four Sunday services, and after every service he would quickly rush off. I asked the Lord to give me an opportunity to talk to this man about his soul's salvation. The next Sunday, he came again. I caught him before he left and asked if I could show him from the Bible what it meant to be a Christian. He agreed. For the next hour we looked into God's Word and God's Word did its work. Before we left that building, he had been saved. Today he is growing in the Lord. When I asked him what brought about the change, he replied, "It was simply God's Word. I just knew when I heard it that it was true." If we are going to fulfill this mission, then we must declare the Word of God in dependence upon the Spirit of God.

If we are going to fulfill this mission, we must declare the Word of God in dependence upon the Spirit of God.

He Gave Us Prayer to God

Prayer alone is not enough, but if we, in obedience to this mandate, are going after souls, we must be praying. Prayer opens doors and softens hearts, preparing souls for the gospel.

Paul said, *"Pray also for us that God would open unto us a door for utterance, to speak the mystery of Christ, for which I am also in bonds: that I may make it manifest, as I ought to speak" (Colossians 4:3-4).*

In 1887, when Jonathan Goforth went to China as a missionary, he was appointed to a new field in the northern section of the province of Honan. Upon learning of Mr. Goforth's assignment, J. Hudson Taylor of the China Inland Mission wrote to say that Northern Honan was the most anti-foreign province in all China. Mr. Taylor said, "They (CIM) tried for ten years to start a work there, but they had not been successful." He gave Mr. Goforth this advice: "You must go forward on your knees."[7] And he did. Eventually Northern Honan became one of the strongest Christian settlements in all of China. God has given us His Spirit, His Word, and direct access to His throne. Our prayers move His hand, which moves the hearts of even the hardest of men.

The Motivation for the Mission *(v. 20b)*

Jesus said, *"Lo, I am with you alway, even unto the end of the world."* What a promise! Wherever you go, the Lord goes. You never go alone. He is with you when you knock on that door or talk to that unsaved person. Jesus goes with you. He always goes with you, and He goes with you everywhere.

Years ago, a missionary found himself in the hands of savage cannibals in Africa. Before the evening meal, by a miracle of God, he escaped and fled into the jungle. Because it was dark and he was in unfamiliar territory, he climbed a tall tree. Looking down, he could see his captors with lighted torches searching the jungle floor for their missing meal. The missionary said, "I never felt Jesus so near as I did that night in the top of that tree." Then he added, "I would go back into that perilous hour if only I could feel again the presence of God with me as I did that dark night."[8]

David Livingstone, that great missionary who opened Africa to the spread of the gospel, one day stood at the headwaters of the Zambezi River. When warned against proceeding farther because of terrible danger, he prayed, opened his Bible, and read *Matthew 28:20: "Lo, I am with you alway, even unto the end of the world."* Accepting God's promise, Livingstone continued on his way to discover Victoria Falls and the eastern outlet from the heart of the Dark Continent.[9]

G. Campbell Morgan was one day reading the Scriptures to female shut-ins in a convalescent home. He read *Matthew 28:20, "Lo, I am with you alway, even unto the end of the world."* He commented, "Isn't that a wonderful promise!" One dear woman replied, "No, it is a reality!" Christ's presence is a reality, not just words in a promise. It is a reality that should motivate us to boldly fulfill this great mission of the church.

Years ago, Hudson Taylor preached in a certain city and led to Christ a Buddhist leader. This new convert, full of joy, asked Mr. Taylor, "How long have you known this good news in your country?" Mr. Taylor answered, "We have had it a long time - several hundred years." "Hundreds of years!" said the ex-Buddhist leader, "and you have never come to tell us? My father sought long and hard for the truth and died without finding it. Oh, Mr. Taylor, why did you not come sooner?"[10] There are people all around crying out for the truth, desiring to possess what we have. It is our mission to reach them.

Today there are 4.5 billion people without Christ. If they could form a single line, it would stretch around the equator twenty-five times. Can you picture twenty-five lines of people, marching endlessly to an eternal hell? [8] We need to declare what we have to those who need what we possess.

Reaching Our Unreached World

Matthew 9:35-38

CHAPTER TEN

Reaching Our Unreached World

Matthew 9:35-38

When the Bible mentions the word nation, it does not generally refer to a political country like France, India, China, or Australia. Rather, it refers to a people-group such as the Serbs of Yugoslavia, the Kurds of Iraq, the Navajo of America, or the Chin of Myanmar.

When Jesus said in *Matthew 28:19, "Go ye therefore, and teach all nations,"* He was not telling us to go to a political country but to an ethnic group - to a people-group. The word "nation" is the Greek word *ethnos*. From it we get the word *ethnic*, which refers to a people-group or an ethnic group. A people-group is defined as any group that has specific characteristics, such as geographical location, language, religion, or culture.

Today there are some 24,000 people-groups in the world. In the last one thousand years, Christians have successfully taken the gospel to 13,000 of these. However, today there are still 11,000 people-groups who have not heard even once the saving gospel of Jesus Christ.[1]

These 11,000 ethnic groups make up roughly 2 billion of the world's population of 6 billion. Out of these 2 billion people, 95 percent live in what is called the 10/40 window. This 10/40 window is the area extending from West Africa to Asia between 10 degrees north and 40 degrees north of the equator. It occupies one-third of the earth's land. Think about this: almost 2 billion people have never heard the gospel, and 95 percent of them live in the 10/40 window.[2]

Christians give approximately 157 billion dollars a year to the work of the church and missions. Of this amount, 94 percent stays at home and 6 percent goes to missions. Out of the 6 percent that goes to missions, only 0.5 percent is designated to reach this 1.9 billion people who have never heard.

Today there are some 308,000 missionaries all across the world. Out of this number only 3,400, or 1.1 percent of the entire mission force is trying to reach this 1.9 billion who have never heard the message of the Cross. This means that in this 10/40 window there is only one missionary - one laborer - for every 5.6 million people.[3]

Why are there so few labourers? When this question was asked to churches and mission agencies, this answer came back: "We cannot effectively work there. The spiritual, political, and economic realities of the 10/40 window seem overwhelming."[4]

When Jesus looked out at the sea of lost humanity almost two thousand years ago, He too was overwhelmed. *Matthew 9:36* says, *"But when He saw the multitudes, He was moved with compassion on them."* But Jesus was not discouraged by the spiritual, political, and economic problems of His day. Instead He tells us how we can reach this lost world and how each of us can be part of world evangelism.

An Acceptance of the Promise *(v. 37a)*

When Jesus looked out over this unsaved world, He said, *"The harvest truly is plenteous."* This was not the first time that Jesus had made this statement. He had declared it three different times in three different places to two different groups of people.

In *John 4:35*, Jesus and His disciples were in Samaria. After Jesus had finished dealing with the woman at the well, He said to His disciples, *"Say not ye, There are yet four months, and then cometh the harvest?"* In making this statement, Jesus was addressing the unbelief of His disciples. He was saying, "You say the harvest is not ready; you say the fields are not yet ripe; you say this place is too hard; you say there needs to be more sowing." *"But I say unto you, 'Lift up your eyes,and look on the fields; for they are white already to harvest.'"*

In *Luke 10:2*, Jesus was across the Jordan River in the area of Perea. This was the most neglected area in the Lord's day. Just before Jesus sent out the seventy to reach this land, He gave them these encouraging words: *"The harvest truly is great."*

Then in our passage, Jesus and His disciples had just finished an intense evangelistic campaign in the area of Galilee. Galilee was an immense area with some three million people in over two hundred cities and villages. As Jesus and His disciples were leaving, He turned and looked at the multitude of unsaved and unreached people and said, *"The harvest truly is plenteous."* Jesus did not say the field is too large or the field is too hard. He said, *"The harvest is plenteous."* In the original Greek no verb is used, and the verse says "The harvest-

There are people right now all around us who are ready to be saved. If we are going to reach these lost souls, then we must accept this promise and realize that this unreached world is ready to be reaped.

plenteous." It speaks of a blunt reality. It lays down for us a fact and gives us a promise that we can stand upon. The reality - the fact - the promise is right now: *"The harvest is plenteous."* It does not matter where a person may be. He could be in Samaria, Perea, or Galilee. He could be in Italy, Iraq, or Iran. He could be in your city, your neighborhood, or your workplace. The blunt reality - the stated fact - the God-given promise is *"the harvest is plenteous."*

There are people right now all around us are ready to be saved. If we are going to reach these lost souls, we must accept this promise and realize that the unreached world is ready to be reaped.

In March of 2000, my wife and I were involved in an evangelistic campaign in Milwaukee, Wisconsin. At the close of meetings, we flew to Chicago, where we were to make our connection to fly to Los Angeles. Our plane from Milwaukee to Chicago was late, so we had to run to catch our connecting flight. We made it to the plane just as they were closing the door. They had already waited fifteen minutes and had decided to leave without us. Since we were the last ones on the plane and the flight was full, there was no room left in the overhead compartments.

We were travelling international, so we had the maximum carry-on luggage. As I struggled to stow our things, all the other passengers were watching me in hot displeasure. The stewardess over the intercom began to say, "Sir, can you please stow your things. Sir, this flight is already late. Sir, there is no room; you are going to have to check those bags."

After fifteen minutes of pure embarrassment, we were on our way. I turned to my wife and said, "Well, you can forget about witnessing to anyone on this flight. After that episode, no one would dare talk to us." There was a lady sitting next to us, probably in her late fifties, who was an auditor for the U.S Navy. My wife began talking to her and was soon sharing the gospel with her. Before long this lady was broken and weeping over her sin. But before Lisa could finish, the plane landed. My wife gave her the gospel tract entitled "Confrontation with Truth," and the lady promised to read it. They exchanged e-mail addresses and parted ways.

Two months later Lisa received an e-mail from this lady named Mary which said, "Hi, Lisa. Don't know if you remember me, but we met coming into L.A. in early March. Well, I kept the pamphlet you gave me, and I followed it through and made the decision. I now believe Jesus has saved me from sin. Thank you for showing me the way." If we are going to reach our world, then we must accept the fact that *"the harvest truly is plenteous."*

I know a man who was a leader in a Baptist church. According to his own testimony, he had ten years of absolute barrenness. He had not memorized a verse of Scripture, he had not witnessed, and he had not won anyone to Christ. Not long ago, the Holy Spirit illumined this truth to him, and he accepted the promise of the harvest. Since that time the Holy Spirit has used him to witness to and to win several hundred people to the Lord. Today he leads the soulwinning training in his church.

One of those trained was a housewife. She too accepted the promise of the harvest and grew burdened to reach the Filipino domestic helpers in her neighborhood. In the afternoons she started going door to door. Within the first few months, she led over fifty Filipinos to the Lord. Many of them enrolled in a Bible study program, were baptized, and joined the church.

The fact is *"the harvest is plenteous,"* and it does not matter whether a person is in the United States, New Zealand, Australia, India, Indonesia, Singapore, or Afghanistan. The harvest is plentiful for those who will accept the promise.

Some say that you cannot expect a harvest in a Buddhist or Islamic country. Some say that you cannot expect to reap souls in a restricted-access nation. I have a missionary friend who went to Vietnam several years ago, which is a restricted-access nation. That means any and all missionary work is forbidden and illegal. Churches and the proclamation of the gospel are not allowed. In spite of the political and spiritual difficulties, in the first two years this missionary won two hundred people to the Lord and started seven house churches. *"The harvest truly is plenteous."*

Several years ago when I was still pastoring in Singapore, I received a phone call from a fellow pastor from Canada. He was on his way to Pakistan and wanted to know if I could meet him at the airport and house him for a few days. When he arrived, I asked him, "Why are you going to Pakistan?" He replied, "To start a church." I then asked whether he knew anyone in Pakistan. He said that he did not. Then I asked, "How do you plan to start a church?" He said, "I will just pick a spot somewhere in the city and start preaching." Three weeks later he returned to Singapore. I again met him at the airport and housed him for a few days before he returned to Canada.

When I asked him about his trip, he said, "I found a street corner, started preaching, and over thirty people were saved." These thirty people gathered together and formed a church. Today, several churches and a Bible college have been started in Islamic Pakistan. The fact is *"the harvest truly is plenteous."*

In December 2001, a group from our church went to Northern Thailand to minister to the Akha. The Akha are still a very primitive tribal people; their culture and lifestyle have not changed in hundreds of years. They live in a large territory that includes the countries of Myanmar, Laos, China, and Thailand. The Akha are animists, extremely superstitious, and heavily involved in demonic worship. One day during the trip our team, which consisted of medical and dental personnel, asked permission to enter a village for the purpose of providing medical and dental services and to preach the gospel of Jesus Christ. Amazingly, the chief of the village allowed them to come in and do as requested. This particular village had never heard the gospel. The chief had never allowed a preacher to enter. The village consisted of one hundred families. Forty people came to the service, and on first hearing of the gospel, fifteen of those present were saved. *"The harvest truly is plenteous."*

Not long ago my wife and I had scheduled a trip to Johannesburg, South Africa. The very morning we were to leave Singapore for South Africa, Lisa fell and ended up with a knot the size of a grapefruit on her left forehead and a swollen-shut right eye. Within a few hours her swollen face was completely black and blue. She was a sight to behold! As we walked together in the airport or on the streets of South Africa, people would look at my wife and then do a double take. Then they would give me a long, hard stare. Before I would begin preaching, I would introduce my wife to the church and then immediately have to say that I was not responsible for her physical condition. One afternoon my wife and the wife of one of the pastors went to the supermarket. As they were walking up the aisle, a Zulu man was stocking the shelves with groceries. He kindly and innocently looked over at my wife and smiled. Then he quickly took a second look and began to stare. When Lisa approached him, he asked with compassion, "Mama, what happened to you?" My wife quickly explained and then turned the conversation to spiritual matters. Within the hour that man was born again.

"The harvest truly is plenteous." If we are going to reach our world, there must be an acceptance of this promise, this blunt reality, this God-inspired fact.

An Awareness of the Problem *(v. 37b)*

Jesus said, *"But the labourers are few."* The problem is not the harvest, for the harvest is ripe. The problem is not the field. The problem is not the sinner. It is not that the lost are too worldly, too wicked, or too sinful to be saved. The problem is not a lack of money and finances. In a similar passage in *Luke 10:2-8*, Jesus sent out the seventy with this admonition: *"Carry neither purse, nor scrip, nor shoes."* If the harvest was dependent upon money, these seventy were in big trouble. The problem is not political turmoil, poor

> *The problem is not political turmoil, poor economic conditions, or the spiritual blindness of the people; these conditions have always existed. The problem is a lack of laborers.*

economic conditions, or the spiritual blindness of the people; these conditions have always existed. The problem is a lack of laborers.

In this 10/40 window there are 1.9 billion people who have never heard even once the message of the cross. There are only 3,400 laborers trying to reach this 1.9 billion. That is one laborer for every 5.6 million people. That's the problem. That's why we are not reaching the world.

People Are Unconcerned

One reason there are so few laborers is that most Christians see the world as a playground instead of a battlefield. People are seen as opportunities but not as eternal souls. Years ago an evangelist and the owner of a city streetcar company were riding down the street together in an automobile. A streetcar loaded to capacity turned the corner and came towards them. "Look!" cried the owner. "A carload of nickels." "A carload of nickels!" replied the evangelist. "I was thinking of a carload of eternal-bound souls."[5] What do you see when you see the multitudes?

In our passage we are told that when Jesus saw the multitudes, *"He was moved with compassion" (v. 36)*. He was moved with compassion because He saw the people as eternal-bound souls. He was moved with compassion because He knew the tragedy of an unreaped harvest.

In the summer of 1839, revival broke out in Dundee, Scotland, under the preaching of William C. Burns, who was filling in for the sick Robert Murray McCheyne. Burns was used greatly in Scotland and later in China to lead multitudes into the kingdom of God. One day in the early part of his ministry,

Burns' mother met him in Glasgow. Seeing him weeping, she asked, "Why those tears?" He answered, "I am weeping at the sight of the multitudes in the streets, so many of whom are passing through life unsaved."[6]

Christians are unconcerned because they have lost sight of the reality of an unreaped harvest. General Booth of the Salvation Army once said that he would like to send all of his candidates for officership to hell for twenty-four hours as the chief part of their training. Why? Because it is not until we have a vital conviction of the irrevocable doom of the impenitent that our belief will crystallize into action.

Have you lost sight of the tragedy of an unreaped harvest? If so, may I suggest that you take your New Testament, turn to *John 3:18*, and meditate on this phrase: *"He that believeth on Him is not condemned."* Remove the *"He"* and place your name there; place your wife's name there; place your child's name there; place your friend's name and your relative's name there. Then take the next phrase, *"He that believeth not is condemned already, because he hath not believed in the name of the only begotten Son of God,"* and with that phrase do the very same thing you did with the first part of the verse and meditate upon it. May God stir you to the reality of an unreaped harvest.

People Are Unbelieving

Not only are Christians unconcerned, they are also unbelieving. Instead of taking God at His Word, they excuse His Word away. Instead of resting upon the promise of the harvest, they give reasons that the harvest is not being reaped. Their excuses go like this: "You cannot reach people here; this area is too Catholic or too Buddhist." "This is an intellectual center;

do not expect much of a response." "These people are too rich and not interested in spiritual things." This is unbelief. Jesus said, *"The harvest truly is plenteous, but the labourers are few."* The problem is not with the unsaved man; it is not with his religion, intellect, or economic level. The problem is the unconcern and unbelief of the saved man.

Many years ago, Charles Peace, a notorious criminal, was brought to justice. Being a burglar, forger, and double murderer, he was condemned to death. As Peace was being led to the scaffold, a chaplain walked by his side, offering what is called "the consolations of religion." As the chaplain spoke of Christ's power to save, the man turned to him and said, "Do you believe it? Do you believe it? If I believed that, I would willingly crawl across England on broken glass to tell men it was true."[7] But it is true! Jesus Christ has the power to save, and He can save any man at any time in any place. He has given us a promise. The harvest truly is plenteous. He has reminded us of the problem but the laborers are few.

An Activation of the Plan *(v. 38)*

Since the harvest truly is plenteous and the laborers are few, what is God's plan for reaching the harvest? What should our response and our responsibility be? How can we bring in the harvest?

Ardent in Prayer *(v. 38)*

The answer is through fervent, urgent, ardent prayer. Jesus says, *"Pray ye therefore the Lord of the harvest, that He will send forth labourers into His harvest."* Reaping the harvest begins with prayer, and there are two important aspects to prayer.

The Priority of Prayer

"Pray ye therefore." This phrase is a command. In the original language, it is an imperative. It is a mandate, a solemn and binding obligation from almighty God to every child of God. So white are the fields, so ripe is the harvest, and so few are the workers that the Lord has commanded we pray for laborers. Prayer is the resource to meet the desperate need. Not only is this a command, it is an urgent command. In the original language, it is in the aorist tense, which means this command is to be obeyed at once.

In the last decade over 1 billion people have left their rural settings and traveled down that concrete highway into the city. Today over 400 cities in the world boast over 1 million in population. Over 300 of those are classified "unevangelized," which means they have had little or no witness for Christ. Casablanca is the most modern city in Morocco. Out of its 4 million people, there are only 400 known evangelical Christians. This is true of all the major cities in northern Africa. Dakar has 1.8 million people, and only 1,260 known Christians. Algiers, the largest city in Algeria, has a population of 3.7 million people and only 2 known Christian fellowships. In Saudi Arabia the city of Mecca has no known Christian. Riyadh, a city of 26 million people, has a few underground believers. Istanbul, with 10 million inhabitants, has only 10 Turkish fellowships. Hanoi, in Vietnam, has a population of 1.2 million and only 7,000 known believers. Phnom Penh, Cambodia, has 2.8 million and only 30 known congregations. In Jakarta, Indonesia, out of 11.4 million people, only 1.4 percent are known Christians. Tokyo/Yokohama has a population of 18.5 million people, and less than one-fourth of one percent are Christians.[8] No wonder this is an urgent command. *"The fields are white unto harvest, but the laborers are few."* The priority is to pray.

The Power of Prayer

"the Lord of the harvest, that He will send forth labourers into His harvest." The result of our praying is God sending forth laborers. The word translated "send forth" is very expressive in the original. It means "to thrust forth." It is the same word rendered "put forth" in *Matthew 9:25* and "cast out" in *Matthew 9:33-34*. It is also in the aorist tense, which implies urgency, promptness, and haste. God commands that we urgently pray, and as a result, God will with the same urgency send forth laborers. It is our responsibility to pray, and it is God's responsibility to send forth laborers.

In *Acts 13:1-2*, Paul and Barnabas found themselves in Antioch. *"As they ministered to the Lord and fasted, the Holy Ghost said, Separate me Barnabas and Saul [Paul] for the work whereunto I have called them."* As the church prayed, the Holy Spirit called Paul and Barnabas and thrust them out into service, and they immediately began their first missionary journey. How are we going to move the hearts of our young people to leave the comforts of home and go to the darkness of heathendom with the message of salvation? What can move the hearts of men for the needs of the world? The answer is prayer. Only the power of God can send forth the needed workers into the harvest field. Our prayers move the hand of God, and God moves the heart of man.

Andrew Murray said, "Prayer is indeed a power on which the ingathering of the harvest and the coming of the kingdom do in very truth depend."[9] If this unreached world is going to be reached, there must be laborers. If laborers are going to be sent, God must send them. If God is going to send them, His people must pray.

It is only through the preaching of the Word that lost souls can hear, and only those who hear can believe, and only those who believe will be saved.

Aggressive in Preaching *(v. 35)*

"And Jesus went about all the cities and villages, teaching in their synagogues, and preaching the gospel of the kingdom." We are to pray that God would send forth laborers and that the laborers would go forth preaching the gospel. Paul said, *"How then shall they call on Him in whom they have not believed? and how shall they believe in Him of whom they have not heard? and how shall they hear without a preacher? And how shall they preach, except they be sent?" (Romans 10:14-15)* As God's people pray, God sends men to preach the Word. It is only through the preaching of the Word that lost souls can hear, and only those who hear can believe, and only those who believe will be saved.

One of the greatest missionary statesmen to ever live was Count Nicolaus von Zinzendorf. No one did more to promote the cause of missions in the eighteenth century than did this German-born nobleman. On August 13, 1727, revival struck the small congregation in Hernhut. As a result, twenty-four men and twenty-four women began a prayer meeting that continued around the clock, seven days a week, without interruption for more than one hundred years. During this hundred-year period this small Moravian congregation sent out more missionaries than did the entire evangelical church in its first one thousand years of existence. They sent missionaries literally everywhere. They went to the West Indies, to the Indians in North America, Alaska, Canada, Greenland, Central and South America, South Africa, India, and the Himalayas. One out of every eight people in this congregation in Hernhut went out to reach the unreached of the day. During the first two years, seventy missionaries flowed from this six hundred member congregation. Twenty-two of these perished in the first two years, and two more were imprisoned, but others took their places. By the time William Carey went to India, over three hundred Moravian missionaries had gone to the ends of the earth. One of these missionaries won to Christ John Wesley, whom God used to ignite the Great Awakening that swept America and Europe. What moved these men and women to leave the comforts and security of their homes? What thrust them out into the harvest fields to reach the lost world? How did they reach their world in their day? The answer can be found in the twenty-four men and the twenty-four women who gathered together to pray. As they prayed, God sent forth laborers, who went forth preaching the gospel of the kingdom.

If we are going to reach this unreached world, God's people must accept the promise: *"The harvest truly is plenteous."* They must be aware of the problem: *"The laborers are few."* And they must activate the plan through ardent prayer and aggressive preaching.

NOTES

Chapter One

[1]J. Oswald Sanders, *The Pursuit of the Holy* (Grand Rapids, Michigan: Zondervan Publishing House, 1972), p. 11.

[2]Ibid., p. 74.

[3]Ruth Paxson, *Rivers of Living Water* (Chicago: Moody Press,1930), pp. 25-26.

Chapter Two

[1]Michael P. Green, *Illustrations for Biblical Preaching* (Grand Rapids, Michigan: Baker Book House, 1991), p. 19.

[2] Bob Whitmore, "Newsworthy," *Frontline Magazine*, May/June 2001, p. 33.

[3] Kent R. Hughes, *Disciplines of a Godly Man* (Wheaton, Illinois: Crossway Books, 1991), pp. 21-22.

[4] Leon Morris, *Tyndale New Testament Commentary: I Corinthians* (Grand Rapids, Michigan: William B. Eerdmans Publishing Company, 1988), p. 93.

Chapter Three

[1]John Phillips, *Exploring Romans* (Neptune, New Jersey: Loizeaux Brothers, 1969), p. 104.

[2]Ibid., p. 106.

[3]Stephen F. Olford, *The Way of Holiness* (Wheaton, Illinois: Crossway Books, 1998), pp. 68-69.

[4]Craig Brian Larson, *Illustrations for Preaching and Teaching* (Grand Rapids, Michigan: Baker Book House, 1993), p. 41.

Chapter Four

[1]J. Oswald Sanders, On to Maturity (Chicago: Moody Press, 1962), p. 152.

[2]Ibid., p. 153.

Chapter Five

[1]Gladys Aylward, *The Little Woman* (Chicago: Moody Press, 1970), p. 8.

[2]J. Oswald Sanders, On to Maturity (Chicago: Moody Press, 1962), p. 55.

Chapter Six

[1]Walter L. Wilson, *Ye Know Him* (Grand Rapids, Michigan: Zondervan Publishing House, 1939), pp. 10-12.

[2]Ibid., pp. 7-8.

[3]Stanley C. Griffin, *A Forgotten Revival* (Bromley, Kent, England: Day One Publications, 1992) pp. 80-81.

[4]Wilson, pp. 10-12..91

Chapter Seven

[1]James A. Stewart, *Our Beloved Jock* (Asheville, North Carolina: Revival Literature, n.d.), p. 32.

[2]R. A. Torrey, *The Person and Work of the Holy Spirit* (Grand Rapids, Michigan: Zondervan Publishing House, 1974), p. 179.

[3]Ted Kyle and John Todd, *A Treasury of Bible Illustrations* (Chattanooga, Tennessee: AMG Pub-lishers, 1995), pp. 213-14.

[4]J. Oswald Sanders, *The Pursuit of the Holy* (Grand Rapids, Michigan: Zondervan Publishing House, 1972), pp. 97-98.

Chapter Eight

[1]J. Oswald Smith, *The Enduement of Power* (London: Marshall, Morgan, and Scott, 1933), pp. 14-15.

[2]William E. Schubert, *I Remember John Sung* (Singapore: Far East Bible College Press, 1976), p. 14.

[3]John R. Rice, *The Sword Book of Treasures* (Murfreesboro, Tennessee: Sword of the Lord Publishers, 1946), pp. 167-69.

Chapter Nine

[1]Donald S. Whitney, *Spiritual Disciplines for the Christian Life* (Colorado Springs, Colorado: Nav-press, 1991), p. 104.

[2]C. Peter Wagner, Stephen Peters, and Mark Wilson, eds., statistics taken from *"Praying Through the 100 Gateway Cities of the 10/40 Window"* (Seattle, Washington: YWAM Publishing, 1995).

[3]Patrick Johnstone, John Hanna, and Marti Smith, eds., statistics taken from *"The Unreached Peoples"* (Seattle, Washington: YWAM Publishing, 1996), pp. 30-31.

[4] Ibid, p. 37.
[5] Rosalind Goforth, *Goforth of China* (Grand Rapids, Michigan: Zondervan Publishing House, 1937), p. 83.
[6] Ibid.
[7] Goforth, pp. 80-81.
[8] W. A. Criswell, *The Holy Spirit in Today's World* (Grand Rapids, Michigan: Zondervan Publish-ing House, 1966), p. 99.
[9] Ibid..92
[10] Howard Taylor, *Biography of James Hudson Taylor* (London: Hodder and Stoughton, 1965), pp. 202-4.

Chapter Ten

[1] C. Peter Wagner, Stephen Peters, and Mark Wilson, eds., Statistics taken from *"Praying Through the 100 Gateway Cities of the 10/40 Window"* (Seattle, Washington: YWAM Publishing, 1995), p. 16.
[2] Ibid.
[3] Ibid, pp. 20-21.
[4] Patrick Johnstone, John Hanna, and Marti Smith, eds., *"The Unreached Peoples"* (Seattle, Washington: YWAM Publishing, 1996), pp. 12-13.
[5] D. Edmond Hiebert. *Working with God through Intercessory Prayer* (Greenville, South Carolina: Bob Jones, University Press, 1991), p. 27.
[6] J. Oswald Sanders. *The Divine Art of Soul Winning* (Chicago: Moody Press, n.d.), pp. 16-17.
[7] Sanders, p. 15.
[8] Wagner, Peters, and Wilson.
[9] Andrew Murray. *With Christ in the School of Prayer* (New York: Grosset and Dunlap, n.d.), p. 58.
[10] J. Robert Morgan. *On This Day* (Nashville, Tennessee: Thomas Nelson Publishers, 1997), August 27.

BIBLIOGRAPHY

Aylward, Gladys. *The Little Woman.* Chicago: Moody Press, 1970.

Criswell, W. A. *The Holy Spirit in Today's World.* Grand Rapids, Michigan: Zondervan Publishing House, 1966.

Goforth, Rosalind. *Goforth of China.* Grand Rapids, Michigan: Zondervan Publishing House, 1937.

Green, Michael P. *Illustrations for Biblical Preaching.* Grand Rapids, Michigan: Baker Book House, 1991.

Griffin, Stanley C. *A Forgotten Revival.* Bromley, Kent, England: Day One Publications, 1992.

Kyle, Ted, and Todd, John. *A Treasury of Bible Illustrations.* Chattanooga, Tennessee: AMG Publishers, 1995.

Hiebert, D. Edmond. *Working with God Through Intercessory Prayer.* Greenville, South Carolina: Bob Jones University Press, 1991.

Hughes, Kent R. *Disciplines of a Godly Man.* Wheaton, Illinois: Crossway Books, 1991.

Johnstone, Patrick; Hanna, John; and Smith, Marti, eds. Statistics taken from *"The Unreached Peoples."* Seattle, Washington: YWAM Publishing, 1996.

Larson, Craig Brian. *Illustrations for Preaching and Teaching.* Grand Rapids, Michigan: Baker Book House, 1993.

Morgan, J. Robert. *On This Day.* Nashville, Tennessee: Thomas Nelson Publishers, 1997.

Morris, Leon. *Tyndale New Testament Commentary: I Corinthians*. Grand Rapids, Michigan: William B. Eerdmans Publishing Company, 1988.

Murray, Andrew. *With Christ in the School of Prayer.* New York: Grosset and Dunlap, n.d.

Olford, Stephen F. *The Way of Holiness*. Wheaton, Illinois: Crossway Books, 1998.

Paxson, Ruth. *Rivers of Living Water.* Chicago: Moody Press, 1930.

Phillips, John. *Exploring Romans*. Neptune, New Jersey: Loizeaux Brothers, 1969.

Rice, John R. *The Sword Book of Treasures*. Murfreesboro, Tennessee: Sword of the Lord Publishers, 1946.

Sanders, J. Oswald. *On to Maturity.* Chicago: Moody Press, 1962.– . *The Divine Art of Soul Winning.* Chicago: Moody Press, n.d.– . *The Pursuit of the Holy.* Grand Rapids, Michigan: Zondervan Publishing House, 1972.

Schubert, William E. I *Remember John Sung.* Singapore: Far East Bible College Press, 1976.

Smith, J. Oswald. *The Enduement of Power.* London: Marshall, Morgan, and Scott, 1933.

Stewart, James A. *Our Beloved Jock.* Asheville, North Carolina: Revival sLiterature, n.d.

Taylor, Howard. *Biography of James Hudson Taylor.* London: Hodder and Stoughton, 1965.

Whitmore, Bob. *"Newsworthy."* Frontline Magazine, May/June 2001.

Whitney, Donald S. *Spiritual Disciplines for the Christian Life.* Colorado Springs, Colorado: Navpress, 1991.

Torrey, R. A. *The Person and Work of the Holy Spirit.* Grand Rapids, Michigan: Zondervan Publishing House, 1974.

Wagner, C. Peter; Peters, Stephen; and Wilson, Mark, eds. Statistics taken from *"Praying Through the 100 Gateway Cities of the 10/40 Window."* Seattle, Washington: WYAM Publishing, 1995.

Wilson, Walter L. *Ye Know Him.* Grand Rapids, Michigan: Zondervan Publishing House, 1939.